Decolonization

The mid-twentieth century experienced the end of the colonial empire, a global phenomenon that left profound changes and created enormous problems contributing to the shape of the contemporary world order and the domestic development of the newly emerging states in the "Third World".

In *Decolonization* Raymond Betts considers this process and its outcomes. Drawing on numerous examples, including those of Ghana, India, Rwanda, and Hong Kong, The author examines the:

- effects of two World Wars on the colonial empire,
- expectations and problems created by independence,
- major demographic shifts accompanying the end of empire,
- cultural experiences, literary movements, and the search for ideology of the dying empire and newly independent nations.

With an annotated bibliography and a chronology of political decolonization, *Decolonization* gives a concise, original, and multi-disciplinary introduction to this controversial theme, and analyzes what the future holds, beyond empire.

Raymond F. Betts is Professor of History at the University of Kentucky. He is author of *France and Decolonization* and *Uncertain Dimensions: Western Overseas Empires in the Twentieth Century.*

The Making of the Contemporary World
Edited by Eric Evans and Ruth Henig
University of Lancaster

The Making of the Contemporary World series provides challenging interpretations of contemporary issues and debates within strongly defined historical frameworks. The range of the series is global, with each volume drawing together material from a range of disciplines – including economics, politics and sociology. The books in this series present compact, indispensable introductions for students studying the modern world.

Other titles in the series include:

Decolonization

Raymond F. Betts

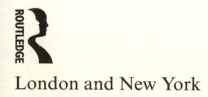

London and New York

First published 1998
by Routledge
11 New Fetter Lane, London EC4P 4EE

Simultaneously published in the USA and Canada
by Routledge
29 West 35th Street, New York, NY 10001

© 1998 Raymond F. Betts

Typeset in Times by
M Rules

Printed and bound in Great Britain by
TJ International Ltd, Padstow, Cornwall

British Library Cataloguing in Publication Data

A catalogue record for this book is available from the British Library

Library of Congress Cataloging in Publication Data

Betts, Raymond F.
    Decolonization / Raymond F. Betts
       p. cm.
    Includes bibliographical references and index.
      1. World politics—1945 2. Decolonization—History. I. Title.
D843.B4856   1988
325'.3'09045—dc21   97-42992
                CIP

ISBN 0–415–15236–4
ISBN 0–415–18682–X (hbk)

To Barbara and Bill, Jean and Gene
for a lifetime of support

Contents

Illustrations

Introduction

"Decolonization" entered the lexicon in the 1930s but did not attain popularity until thirty years later. It is an awkward and inelegant word, therefore, in a way, appropriate to the subject it attempts to describe. Unlike the phrase "end of empire" which has a certain poetic economy suggesting a grand and sweeping occurrence, "decolonization" is work-a-day, rather like other "de" prefixed words that denote cleansing changes.

Decolonization was not a process but a clutch of fitful activities and events, played out in conference rooms, acted out in protests mounted in city streets, fought over in jungles and mountains. Its results pleased no one. It was too hastily done for some, too slowly carried out for others, too incomplete in effect for most. The subject is historically loose-ended; there is no end to discussion of it. Not only does the old historical problem of mechanical physics here arise again – the question of whether the European colonial empires were overthrown or collapsed because of their own weight – but continuing problems of political and social exploitation in the contemporary world beg this question: are these, too, the outcomes of decolonization as a failed exercise in the transfer of power and nation-building?

One matter is certain: in the political sense of the word, decolonization is over and done with. The exceptional moment announcing the fact occurred at midnight on June 30, 1997, the beginning of the first day of Hong Kong's reversion to China after a century-and-a-half of British control. The occasion was surrounded by several days of lavish parties, displays of resplendently attired honor guards, and many speeches. Particular events were the departure of the last British governor from the official residence in his Rolls-Royce sedan in a three-time turn of the circular drive as an expression of Chinese good luck and then a $13 million, hour-long fireworks extravaganza projected over Victoria Harbour. The diverse activities of the handover ceremony were also celebrated, as had been no other expression of decolonization, worldwide on more than 22,000 websites. Never before has the finality of a political condition been so colorfully and dramatically enacted and so widely recorded.

What now remains of overseas empire is inconsequential, in appearance rather like shards of pottery indifferently cast on distant shores. Tahiti, still French, and Bermuda, still British, are arguably the only two colonial possessions that still occupy some small part of the popular imagination, largely because of the exoticism attributed to each. Yet with a combined population of 201,000 and a combined land surface of 435 square miles, they add up to little in contemporary world affairs. Other small islands have been absorbed as integral parts of the nation state that once controlled them as colonies. Such is true of the Netherlands Antilles, and of Guadeloupe and Martinique, now French departments.

Elsewhere, the old imperial possessions now stand as sovereign states, over a hundred of them, thus accounting for the vast majority of the members – currently 158 – in the United Nations. Of great interest is the fact that most of the colonial-imposed political boundaries have been respected. Belize, for instance, is old British Honduras, its name, not its shape changed; and the Democratic Republic of the Congo, despite its recent tumultuous condition when it was known as Zaire, is still the land mass it was as the Belgian Congo. The major exception, is, of course, India, from which Pakistan separated at independence from Great Britain in 1947, with a further split occurring in 1971 when Bangladesh seceded from Pakistan.

The political history of decolonization has been extensively reviewed and presented in a number of all-embracing, overarching texts. The small study that here follows diverges somewhat from the standard. There will be little attention given to political parties and to international accords. There will be considerable attention directed to environment and atmosphere, to the sense of place, space, and perspective. The effort will be to provide a meaningful landscape of change, framed by some five decades, the span from 1918 to 1963, from the end of World War I to the independence of Kenya, one of the last of the major colonial territories to become a sovereign state.

Modern colonial empire provides an unusual history of small numbers of people lording it over large masses and widely scattered groups, the relationship always fragile and uncertain, yet outwardly given the appearance of solidarity and certainty by pomp and circumstance. Consider this one telling statement by Norman Leys, an English colonial medical officer who assessed the demographic condition of Kenya in his general study, *Kenya* (1921), when the indigenous population was slightly over 2 million and the European population was 9,651: "The whole European colony . . . is no more than equal to the population of a large street in a European city." Now consider one of the last moments of regal ceremony when the governor of Kenya greeted Princess Elizabeth and her husband Prince Philip on February 1, 1952, as the young couple arrived at Nairobi, the first stop of a planned Commonwealth tour. (Kenya had long been advertised as a place for the rich and high born to vacation in the winter months.) There, at the airfield, in attendance on the royal visitors, was the governor dressed in colonial whites, bearing a ceremonial sword and coifed with a colonial pith helmet above which ostrich feathers, long the symbol of high rank, fluttered.

Empire was as much stage performance as military engagment, as much the presentation of arms as the firing of them – as so many contemporary historians have remarked. The several trips that the Prince of Wales, the future King Edward VIII, made around the British empire right after World War I were showpieces of imperial unity. The appearance of African troops, along with units of the Foreign Legion, at the annual Bastille Day parade down the Champs Elysées in Paris served the same purpose. In the colonies themselves the Europeans frequently supported or even created rituals of power for local rulers whose cooperation they sought and needed. Titles conferred, medals awarded, military training provided – such acts as these were designed both to confer new authority on the local ruler and to force his embrace of European colonial empire.

To state this is not to suggest that repressive measures taken by colonial governments and expressions of bitter dissatisfaction made by Asian and African leaders will be ignored in the text. Empire was a precarious balance of fact and intention. And so the text will attempt to combine, in meaningful narrative, commentary on the lie of the land as well as on the frame of mind.

Decolonization was first the subject of political historians and political scientists who viewed the activity as either a national or an international problem, one of party formation, mass protest, nation building, big state rivalry. Decolonization still remains a subject of concern to social scientists, but it has more recently figured prominently in literary criticism, itself informed by cultural anthropology, the new hybrid most frequently described as colonial or postcolonial discourse, with "discourse" meaning not only language but the cultural conditions that inform and direct it. Decolonization thus implies for some critics changes of attitude and mentality in both of those communities once simply defined as "home" and "abroad."

Perhaps this extended occurrence and the debate over it, both subsumed under the word "decolonization," can best be summarized in a spontaneous but symbolic gesture. It occurred, most appropriately, as European political rule in Africa was quickly terminating. The scene, photographed and made into the cover picture of *Life* magazine for July 11, 1960, serves to illustrate the theme of this book. There, in Leopoldville, Belgian Congo (soon to be Kinshasa, Zaire), an African student can be seen melodramatically and gleefully stealing the ceremonial sword of King Baudouin of the Belgians as the king's convertible automobile (as meticulously black as the king's colonial uniform is spotlessly white) moves forward in solemn procession.

The king is oblivious to what has just happened.

Others were not. The subject of decolonization was then, and now continues to be, one of intense scholarly interest. The text that follows is an attempt to show the dimensions and to explain the course of that phenomenon so significant to contemporary global history.

1 Empire in the afternoon

The interwar years

Only twice in the twentieth century did colonial empire acquire the unity and grandeur that its proponents desired. Both occasions were expositions, held in the capital cities of the two greatest imperialist powers of the time: Great Britain and France. The British Empire Exposition of 1924 was held in Wembley Park in London; the International Colonial Exposition was held in 1931 in the Bois de Vincennes in Paris. Each exposition was an elaborate effort to display and advertise empire as colorfully varied but purposefully well ordered. Miniaturized and sanitized, each gave the viewer the immediate illusion of a whole that exceeded the sum of its parts, a worldwide enterprise of divergent peoples and ecologically different territories brought together under one flag for the declared benefit of colonizer and colonized alike. As the brochure for the British Empire Exposition announced, "There the visitor will be able to inspect the Empire from end to end."

The seeming order of it all, the impressive but easily encompassed reality of it all (170 Chinese workers were to be found at the Hong Kong section which took "the form of an exact reproduction of a street in Hong Kong") on the 216 acres of London park serving as a local expression of the one-quarter of the globe then under British control, suggested rather enduring and well-structured form. The French International Colonial Exposition was an even grander effort to express a lesser colonial empire, laid out across 500 acres. With one of its principal buildings designed to be the permanent Museum of Colonies, the French planners made a public and most visible statement of historical intent. A bas-relief that ran around the building depicted the French colonial world and, at 1,200 square meters in total length, was the largest such sculpture ever executed, an artistic expression of the imagined place France occupied in the world and in modern history.

These two expositions suggested the first of the two principal perspectives from which colonial empire was measured and assessed. Seen at a great distance, which was from the detached metropolitan view of things, the enormous diversity of cultures, people, and environments was given an orderly yet dramatic assembly that was happily wondered at. On the neatly landscaped grounds of Wembley the visitor was invited to tour the world "at a minimum of cost, in a minimum of time, with a minimum of trouble, studying as you go the shop windows of the British Empire," or so stated the official brochure.

The second perspective was the close-at-hand view of things, shaped by the experience of the local colonial official, the British "district officer" or the French *commandant*, the person given the administrative responsibility for maintaining the *pax colonia*, that so-called colonial peace which primarily consisted of assuring order and collecting taxes. This dual activity was not done single-handedly, of course. There was need of collaborators, of locals with power (tribal chiefs and mandarins) and influence (merchants and traders). Their positions now being maintained and reinforced by the European officers, these individuals stood to benefit from the colonial experience. Equally significant were the interpreters who translated the commands and wishes of the Europeans, along with complaints and requests of the local population. Even though all of the colonial powers had established schools for training administrators, the language gap was an important one in preventing understanding and in confusing purpose.

Generally assuming what has been called an "enclave mentality," the Europeans in the colonial territories remained socially and geographically separated from the indigenous peoples, and therefore seldom encouraged a meeting of minds. In his novel, *A Passage to India* (1924), E. M. Forster describes a "bridge party" arranged so that the two women visitors from England, who are also central characters of the story, may meet "real" Indians, as they had desired. The two groups stand apart facing each other on the lawn, perhaps thirty feet apart physically but separated culturally by an immeasurable distance. Whether in India or Indochina, Senegal or Somaliland, the unbridged distance was great. If European colonial attitudes toward the colonized varied, they usually ranged narrowly between undisguised contempt and romantic condescension. The term "native," now so derisive in connotation, was then a descriptive term of the essence of the colonial world which consisted of objects to be viewed, examined, and cataloged as part of a particular setting. In this sense anthropologists and administrators were as one: concerned with living among but standing apart from the peoples they officially encountered. In the process they defined themselves and their own culture in a negative manner, as not being what the colonized people were, as being distinct from what the local cultures "demonstrated." Popular terms to describe one or the other were: childlike, primitive, superstitious, irresponsible. The Europeans were seen, by themselves, as beneficially contrary. When Norman Leys, a British medical officer, wrote of his experiences in Kenya in the first decade of the twentieth century, he said that the two great contributions of the British to Africa were the railroad and the hall of justice. Cultural advancement and order, the much vaunted ideals of Europe before World War I, were what the Europeans thought they were providing the rest of the world.

The rhetoric of imperialism as expressed in book prefaces and after-dinner speeches was regularly cast on a high plane. No one better summed up the imperial ideal than did Lord Curzon, Viceroy of India between 1899 and 1905, whose language was only matched by his resplendent appearance in his official portrait as viceroy. In a speech given in Birmingham in 1908, he spoke of empire as an "inspiration" and then asserted that empire must give to "the people on the circumference . . . what they cannot otherwise or elsewhere enjoy; not merely justice or order, or material prosperity, but the sense of partnership in a great idea."

That idea was European rule, declared to be beneficent and usually summarized for home consumption in one of two terms: "civilizing mission" or "White man's burden," the latter being the title of Rudyard Kipling's famous poem (1899) which was directed by the English poet to the Americans as commentary of what they must do and might expect as they assumed responsibility in the newly conquered Philippine Islands.

From our contemporary perspective such terms and the notions they embraced are abhorrent. They are at best pretentious and at worst racist. They further express the peculiar geography of imperialism wherein Europe was the center of world affairs. In simple cultural geometry, the world consisted of two vast circles, a core and a periphery (Curzon's "circumference"). From the core, Western Europe, radiated outward those attributes we describe today as "modern." They were defined as technological, organizational, and rational. They were displayed in modern cities with efficient transportation systems, in parliamentary government and capitalist corporations, in university degrees and scientific research, in the market system and the industrial process. The French critic and novelist Pierre Mille caustically remarked on this attitude in 1905 that "the Chinese, having no railroads, mechanical textile machinery, no Napoleon and no Moltke, are extremely inferior to us." As he obviously implied, the link between technological advancement and cultural superiority was easily made.

That superiority was also assumed to be timely, an expression of historical circumstances. The expression "advanced" as a term descriptive of the condition of European civilization was synonymous with "forward," the position in which the Europeans placed themselves in the march of time. This condition is what Joseph Conrad had accepted in *Heart of Darkness* (1902), when the narrator Marlow comments parenthetically about the Africans aboard his ship heading up the Congo:

> I don't think a single one of them had any clear idea of time, as we at the end of countless ages have. They still belonged to the beginning of time – had no inherited experience to teach them as it were.

Marlow speaks, as today's post-modernist critics would argue, as the master narrator, the individual of the culture which considered all of humankind linearly arranged – through ages, periods, and times – from still obscure beginnings to the now, the "modern," of the enlightened Western condition and ideal. ("Darkness" and "light" were the extremes, and this visual metaphor, so ironically and heavily used by Conrad in his famous novella, was commonplace in the rhetoric of empire.) As the world was thus made to converge on the European present, its configurations, its meaning and purpose were determined by the Europeans as well. The Europeans had a "planetary consciousness," an awareness of global proportions and a desire to define what they saw and encountered.[1] They were the "discoverers" who established the dimensions and the measures of whatever fell before their gaze – or under their boot. The names and nomenclature were European: French Guinea and the Belgian Congo, Mount Cook (New Zealand), and Victoria Falls (Zimbabwe); protectorates (the form of French rule over Tunisia and, briefly, of British rule over British East Africa, to become Kenya in 1920); and federations (French Indochina and the Federated Malay States). The point of view was European: the "maidan" as a grassy line of division between English and indigenous residential areas in urban centers; the governor-general's palace in Dakar on the "plateau," the high land overlooking the sea and the city; the *Litoranea Libica*, the grand coastal road constructed by the Fascists in Libya and inaugurated by Benito Mussolini in a motorcade in 1937.

Even the history itself was European: discoveries and explorations came from without and with them came the assumption that the "modern" phase of history was initiated by the Europeans. "Precolonial" was a popular descriptive adjective for "before," and it frequently contained the assumption of the rudimentary and the primitive. More than one author went so far as to assert that African history began with the arrival of the Europeans. Even to this day something of that peculiar cultural consciousness that allowed easy division of the world into the English dualism of "home" and "abroad"[2] or the French of *métropole* and *territoires d'outre-mer* is found in the American academic custom of lumping all of history that is neither American nor European into the category of "non-Western."

In an obvious way the two colonial expositions discussed in this chapter can be seen as narratives of power, the arrangement of lands and peoples according to European purposes and principles. The arrangement was of viewer and viewed, of dominant and dominated, of colonizer and colonized. Both expositions offered visions of a world constructed by Europeans and obtaining its meaning in those terms alone. Here were the British empire and the French overseas empire, the national adjectives standing as the exclusive determinants. And here in temporary buildings on two sites far removed from colonial lands was declared testimony of a European-dominated world. "French expansion," wrote Pierre Lyautey in a book (*L'Empire colonial français*) printed on the occasion of the French colonial exposition, "is durable and permanent." The tautology only reinforced his argument.

Even though World War I had shattered many illusions about progress and Europe's assumed justifiable supremacy, the significant changes in attitudes toward colonies were much more of tone and temper than of purpose. Grafted to the older idea of "civilizing mission" was the newer one of needed colonial economic development for the benefit of all humankind. Strident nationalist arguments were replaced by an international sentiment in part engendered by a recognition in Great Britain and France of the contribution of the colonies to the war effort, as the suppliers of manpower and goods. Yet still affirmed were those conditions that are most easily appreciated in the contemporary literary term "binary opposition." The metropolitan country and the colonial regions formed contrasts in European eyes: the one considered to be "advanced," as determined by its high degree of organization, technology, and skill; the other seen as "backward," as evidenced by its rudimentary or decadent forms of government, its unproductive way of doing things, its lack of the skills, motivation, and level of cultural attainment necessary to generate economic development. One of the statements most clearly expressing this binary opposition was that made in 1931 by Pierre Ryckmans, soon to be governor of the Belgian Congo (1934–60). His words were addressed to a group of young lawyers in Brussels: "What we must overcome in order to make the Black [African] work is not so much his laziness as his disdain for *our* concept of work, his indifference to *our* concept of wages."[3] Residing within this remark are all the conditions which critics of

European imperialism would later denounce: a barely disguised racism; a blanket treatment of the "other," of an imagined collectivity here expressed in the collective personal noun, "the Black"; of disdain or disrespect for other cultures; of an assumption that history, considered as the forward march of progress, sided with the Europeans, as suggested in the originally underlined personal possessive "ours." Put otherwise, modern European imperialism was unidirectionally driven toward European needs and intentions in thought such as this, the thought of those who supported empire.

Armed with such thought, few persons who considered the colonial situation ever enquired, as did King George V, whose last recorded and only memorable words were: "How is the Empire?"

The answer, as we now know, ought to have been "going, going, gone." But hindsight is the wisdom of historians, not of the actors and thinkers of the time. In 1924 and again in 1931 the imperial enterprise seemed quite secure. And it certainly was widely and unabashedly celebrated. The United States was dotted with movie and vaudeville theaters named "empire" and "imperial," while the Chrysler Motor Company gave new motion to the concept when it named its new, top-of-the-line model "Imperial" in 1931. Out West, in the far reach of the American continental empire, Hollywood encouraged the establishment of an English settlement colony of sorts for those actors in the escapist movies of the 1930s who were so successful at playing duty-bound sergeants-major, resolute colonels, and, occasionally, generals with bushy eyebrows supposedly grown from the experience of battlefield command in the northern passages of India or across the vast sweep of the Arabian Desert. Never was loyalty to the imperial idea affirmed with greater resolution than when Shirley Temple in the film version of Kipling's short story *Wee Willie Winkie* (1935) stood at attention and announced her devotion to Queen and empire, no matter that empire was strictly a male affair and that Kipling's little hero was just that, a young boy.

What was projected on the movie screen was also newly mapped out with global air routes. Enthusiasts expected empire to be more closely and quickly bound together by such companies as KLM, Air France, and British Imperial Airways, all in operation by the 1930s. The overly optimistic Lord Thomson, British minister of air in 1931, embarked on what he considered a new and luxurious service from west to east, from a mooring mast at Cardington, north of London, to another in Karachi, then part of British India. Between the two, the imperially proportioned airship R-101 (777 feet in length) would make its progress, laden with Lord Thomson's ample luggage, with champagne and fine china to allow a banquet aboard at Ismailia, an intermediate touch-down point in the journey. Seven hours out on its maiden flight and only 300 miles along the way, the R-101 crashed and burned in woods just outside Beauvais, France. The airship and the tragic event are com-memorated by a stone marker.

The prophet, rather than the historian, might have read into the fate of the R-101 that of empire: huge, underpowered, flimsy in construc-tion, hollow within, ill-directed, and soon to crash. But such an interpretation would be falsely prescient. Empire showed few signs of structural weakness in the interwar period.

In truth, the physical dimensions of the colonial world reached their largest scope in this era. World War I resulted in the defeat of the German and Ottoman empires and their debris was added to the British and French colonial empires and to the Belgian as well. On the other side of the world, the outcome of the war even allowed Australia and New Zealand to engage in a sort of sub-imperialism as they picked up island parts of the former German oceanic empire. Through the man-dates system initiated by the Peace Conference at Versailles and instituted within the League of Nations, territories including Syria, Palestine and Lebanon, former German East Africa (Tanganyika), Southwest Africa, and Togo and Cameroon were placed under new colonial administration. Article 22 of the League Covenant spoke of a "sacred trust" that the mandatory powers had to respect and initiate through the betterment of these territories for the benefit of their resi-dent populations. Article 3 of the mandate to Great Britain and Belgium over former German East Africa read:

the Mandatory shall be responsible for the peace, order and good government of the territory, and shall undertake to promote to the utmost the material and moral well-being and social progress of its inhabitants.

Moreover, the official intention of all the mandates was that of guidance toward self-rule. Little of the sort was achieved, and Cameroon, divided in mandate between the French and the English, was soon treated as if a regular colonial territory which was what most of the supporters of colo-nial empire wanted. Rather than enthusiastically support the mandates system, they merely tolerated it in order to silence the anti-colonial rhetoric of the American President Woodrow Wilson. Prime Minister Lloyd George of Great Britain attempted, albeit unsuccessfully, to get the United States to assume a mandate. He did so with the thought that the Americans and their idealistic President Woodrow Wilson would thus be denied "any prejudice against us on the ground of 'land grabbing'."

Such language as that of Lloyd George did not accompany public pronouncements or major policy decisions made at the time. "Empire" had replaced "imperialism" in the established lexicon. Whereas the British had used the term with pride and flair for some time, it now also became popular in France. It was even given official sanction by the Italians in 1936, when, after the conquest of Ethiopia, the government adopted the term *Impero* (and shortly thereafter gave the name to a new battleship). The Italian conquest may be seen as a glaring exception because empire now meant to its proponents economic development and political responsibility more than anything else. The term "domination," used rather unhesitatingly before World War I, was now generally replaced by "dependency." The latter term suggested a beneficial relationship in which one party helped the other. It was, perhaps, given its most significant definition by Sir Frederick Lugard in his famous study, *The Dual Mandate in Tropical Africa*, first published in 1922. According to Lugard, the European presence in Africa had allowed raw materials which "lay wasted and ungarnered . . . because the natives did not know their use and value" to be made available to Europeans, while the Africans received from the Europeans in turn "the substitution of law and order for the methods of barbarism." The result of this activity, he asserted, "can be made reciprocal, and that is the aim and desire of civilized administration to fulfill this dual mandate." Economic development and cultural development, such was the simple sum of Lugard's argument about the "dual mandate." The French minister of colonies, Albert Sarraut, echoed similar sentiments in his work *La Mise en valeur des colonies françaises (The Economic Development of the French Colonies)*, published in 1923:

> The France that colonizes does not do so for itself: its advantage is joined with that of the world; its effort, more than for itself, must be of benefit to the colonies whose economic growth and human development it must assure.

Such conceits as these, while widely accepted with either nonchalance or indifference, were critically contested by a small but vocal number of individuals in interwar Europe as well as abroad. Not only was the colonial enterprise itself cast in doubt but the civilization that made it possible was questioned. Perhaps the two most celebrated fictional dissents were both published in the 1920s. The first was written by René Maran, a Black author originally from the Caribbean island of Martinique. Published in 1921, *Batouala* won the coveted Goncourt Literary Prize in 1922, some indication of the novel's cultural impact. Set in Africa, *Batouala* recounts the life of its chief character under

French colonial rule. The author's prefatory note is stern; it turns the notion of the torch of French civilization (consider the official title of the Statue of Liberty, a French construction: "Liberty Enlightening the World") into something of a device for scorching the earth: "You are not a torch," he exclaims, "but a fire. Whatever you touch, you consume."

Using an entirely different metaphor, E. M. Forster in *A Passage to India,* published in 1924, reaches a similar conclusion. All the effort at unity of purpose and spirit between the English and the Indians, what Forster described metaphorically as overarching, only resulted at the apex in silence. All below was lost in confusion and misunderstanding. The novel ends as two of the characters, one English and the other Indian, are riding together on horseback when the one asks of the other, "Why can't we be friends?" At that moment, the horses part ways because of a large boulder in the path. This action was, as Forster writes, an indication that the understanding and appreciation which assure friendship among different peoples was still impossible. The horses "did not want it," he simply states. Nor did anything else in that colonial environment want or expect it, he insists: "'No, not yet,' and the sky said, 'No, not there'." With these words the novel closes, suggesting that the colonial experience was doomed to failure, being at best an exercise in good intentions based on false premises.

To rephrase the well-known line of poetry written by William Butler Yeats, one may say that things did not fall apart in the colonial world. They had never come harmoniously together except in speeches and writings of a pro-imperialist tenor and, of course, on the exposition grounds of Wembley and the Bois de Vincennes. To radical critics of the colonial situation, however, there was a brutal alliance of sorts, a forced situation of exploitation in which imperialism was a term of forceful domination. This was the basic assumption informing the arguments made from the left in the interwar years when Communism, now with an institutional base in the new Soviet Union (1917) and an institutional propaganda arm, the Third International or Comintern (1919), made compelling the analogy between exploiting capitalist and exploited worker and exploiting imperialist nation and exploited colonial people. Imperialism, in this global scheme of things, was rapacious capitalism expanded overseas in a desperate search for new markets and resources to command, other people to oppress, all motivated by the desire for investment opportunities and subsequent profit. Vladimir Lenin had given this idea a patina of literary credibility in his *Imperialism, The Highest Stage of Capitalism* (1920), in which he heavy-handedly arranged statistics and historical developments to affirm that modern imperialism not only coincided with but was largely precipitated by finance capitalism looking for lucrative places of investment, now that home markets were saturated. This tract was set up in academic abstractions and outfitted with economic tables to provide the semblance of a critical mass. More striking in tone and effect was the first major publication of Nguyên-Aï-Quôc, the future Vietnamese leader Ho Chi Minh, who drew up and had published in 1926 a strong and bitter indictment of French imperialism, entitled *Le Procès de la colonisation* (*Colonization on Trial*). The grievances listed included examples of brutal treatment, cultural arrogance, and economic exploitation. One of Nguyên's conclusions concerned the sham of empire: "To hide the ugliness of its criminally exploitative regime, colonial capitalism always decorates its rotten shield with the idealistic device: Fraternity, Equality, etc."

A young radical, resident in France in 1923, Ho returned to Indochina by way of the Soviet Union and China. In 1925 he founded the Vietnamese Young League of Revolutionaries. He was one of many persons so engaged in such activities of protest and reform in the interwar years. Hardly a colony was without a political organization giving vent to such expressions; and many future first presidents of the new nations transformed from the old colonies entered the political stage by first serving in such organizations in the interwar years: men like Jomo Kenyatta in Kenya, Habib Bourguiba in Tunisia, Sukarno in Indonesia, and Jawaharlal Nehru in India.

Action was frequently inspired or accompanied by such organizations and by the means of local expression, the newspaper. Militant parties, demanding either freedom or fundamental reform, appeared just about everywhere, but most strongly in North Africa and Asia. The Neo-Destour Party in Tunisia, a 1934 offshoot of the earlier Destour (Constitutional) Party, demanded immediate independence and started demonstrations sufficiently large and vocal to disturb the French. A few years later, in 1937, the able and ambitious Nigerian Nnamidi Azikiwe founded the *West African Pilot,* arguably the most renowned of newspapers from the colonial era and which, while not radical in its formative year, stated in its initial editorial that its program was "based on the quest for social justice."

These two significant examples show that the well-landscaped, peaceful, and praised imperial scenes noticeable at Wembley in 1924 or the Bois de Vincennes in 1931 were contrasted by the discordant notes heard and the agitation seen in the colonial possessions themselves. The historical truth is that there had always been opposition, armed resistance, whenever and wherever the Europeans disembarked or moved inland in the age of overseas expansion. There were protests against mass relocation to make property available to Europeans; there was outright opposition to taxes, such as the "hut tax wars" in Africa. And there were strikes: 98 in Indochina in 1930 alone, with some 31,000 participants in all. And there were major acts of rebellion, of which that of the Rif War in Morocco (1921–6), led by the resourceful Abd-el-Krim, was one of the most significant and long drawn out in the interwar era (and the only one celebrated in song, in the American musical, *Desert Song*).

"Pacification" was the euphemism employed to describe the police and military action required of the colonial powers to maintain their positions. As the old saying goes, empire was won and maintained by the sword. And so it was throughout its modern history. One of the most commented on expressions of such repressive measures was the massacre at Amritsar in the Punjab region of India in 1919. As an expression of protest against British rule, some 5,000 supporters of the Indian National Congress, now demanding *swaraj* (home rule) under the leadership of Mohandas Gandhi, gathered in defiance of an order against such gatherings by the local military commander, Brigadier Dyer. Dyer, with a company of soldiers, arrived and commenced firing on the crowd and did so until his men ran out of ammunition. There were 379 persons killed and some 1,200 were wounded. The wanton act left a deep mark on Indians and raised new questions about the British concept of order and justice.

Other repressive measures were taken against the uprisings, some communist inspired, that were most evident in Asian reaches of empire. The Dutch put down revolts in Java and Sumatra in 1926–7. The French did likewise in Indochina in 1930. What was perhaps most significant about the repression of this particular nationalist upheaval from the empire perspective was the appearance before the presidential palace in Paris of a crowd of angry Vietnamese students numbered at 1,556. Thus, a year before the French colonial exposition laid out the order of empire in the Bois de Vincennes, its disorder was briefly demonstrated across town before the presidential palace.

In face of such unsettling developments in their colonial world, the Europeans were not serenely indifferent or contemptuously dismissive. Tempered confidence might be the best expression of the general attitude. Sarraut, in the volume already cited, briefly worried about increase "of agitation among the colored races" that he felt were expressions of agitation "not without danger for European civilization." And both France and Great Britain were fretful about their hold on their possessions in the Pacific as Japan grew to be a world power anxious to create in Southeast Asia a "Co-prosperity Sphere," the latest in euphemisms for imperialism.

Yet almost all who observed and commented, favorably or otherwise, assumed that empire would be a global fixture for some time to come. The director of the French Colonial School, Georges Hardy, made a remark supportive of this idea as he sweepingly surveyed modern colonization in 1937 and concluded that Europe, barring catastrophe, "is far from having exhausted its resources of endurance." And even in the middle of that catastrophe which was World War II, Margery Perham, a well-known colonial authority and significantly the wife of Lord Lugard, wrote in her book *Africa and British Rule* (1941) that "Africans must have foreign rulers, and for a long time to come."

If there was a growing tolerance, even encouragement of diversity in "native policy," it was now informed by anthropological research which encouraged respect for local customs and regional ecologies. The thought of a unified empire, a well-constructed mosaic of particular pieces, was still desired by many. Empire was for these individuals to be something more than a rhetorical device. It suggested a source of national greatness that was reassuring at a time of domestic strife and division, as indeed were the decades of the 1920s and 1930s in Europe. The French International Colonial Exposition may thus be seen as a visible statement of that unity in diversity. Beautifully arranged and carefully articulated, it stood as a simulacrum, a briefly presented reality of what was imagined to be.

The reality of the matter did not extend beyond the exposition grounds, however. Understaffed, underfunded, and never well understood, the units of colonial empire were only unified in intention, seen as sources of economic strength and of political power and, in a complementary way, as depositories of European culture. They were those places where "some real work is done" – to use Marlow's appraisal of British activities in Africa as expressed in *Heart of Darkness*.

More significantly, empire was not considered in popular thought to be a crucial national or international issue until after World War II when the then waning colonial powers thought they found in empire their particular source of renewable global strength. Nor did matters of empire ever occupy parliamentary attention in any European nation on a regular basis. In the prewar era and continuing through the interwar period, matters of empire required concentrated thought only when budgetary considerations were debated.

Worldwide in geographical fact, colonial empire was insular in terms of national affairs. It was politically distanced from the major issues of

European international politics. More collaborative than conflicting, the European colonial powers never allowed issues among themselves to heat up to battlefield temperatures. The one dramatic scene of tense encounter occurred outside the Sudanese city of Fashoda in 1898 when a French expeditionary force, newly arrived there, was met by a far more formidable English force under the generalship of Lord Kitchener (whose face gained wide recognition later when featured on recruitment posters during World War I). What might have been a provocation of war, in which each side claimed rights of territorial possession, was quickly settled by diplomatic negotiation. The only major colonial wars in the era of expansion were between Europeans and "others": the Italian–Abyssinian War of 1896 in which the Italians were defeated; the Russo–Japanese War of 1904–5 in which the Russians were defeated. Somewhat anomalous was the Spanish–American War of 1898 which was an obvious conflict between an old European colonial power and the major New World power that had itself begun as a set of colonies. As exceptions that proved the rule, these wars were exterior to the European-regulated colonial system wherein rhetorical bluster was never matched by artillery salvoes.

Even in the interwar period, when disturbances in places like India and Morocco were front-page news, colonial empire was generally treated by the public as an incidental fact of life, seeming to be as much a part of the order of things as were carved pineapples as finials on furniture; tea taken in the late afternoon; and the weekly "boat days," those festive occasions which marked the arrival of steamships in the ports of the Pacific. (The Aloha Tower in Hawaii, constructed in the interwar period to serve as a focal point of arrival in Honolulu, still brightly displays its welcoming word at night in this air age.)

Put it this way: empire was like Nelson's statue in Trafalgar Square or the Eiffel Tower on the Champs de Mars – it was just there. It was a source of national pride to those who attended the expositions of 1924 and 1931. It was a source of entertainment to those who attended the movies. It was a source of tales of daring and of fables about jungle animals (the elephant Babar, of course) that excited, if they did not educate, young children. And it appeared in an indirect but familiar way in the products that used a colonial logo, as did the French breakfast food Banania with its prominently displayed Senegalese sharpshooter saying, "Y'a c'st bon" (perhaps best translated as crudely in English as it appears in French as "Dat's good"). If, as critics have commented, the vast majority of British, French, Belgians, and Dutch were ignorant of the facts of empire, they nonetheless held sentiments about it. A minority of the public was vigorously opposed, but a majority was casually and contentedly supportive. Against the detailed expressions of contempt and cynicism provided by the first group appeared the fuzzy sentiment of the other, that of simply feeling good about it.

Most Europeans would, if required, have asserted something similar to the statement once humorously made by the French senator Lucien Hubert: "The colonies, well, they are something far away, out there, in broad sunlight."[4]

2 The sea change of empire
The effects of World War II

The title of this chapter seems most appropriate. The metaphor is taken from Shakespeare's *The Tempest*, whose setting of an island shipwreck was based on an early colonial adventure which did in fact end in that lamentable condition. More significant is the broad characteristic of modern colonial empire as seaborne, a geographical condition suited, if at all, to that first phase of industrialization when the European world was powered by steam and structured with iron and steel. Some easily found statistical proof of this contention is found in *Lloyd's Register* (1910–11) which indicated that Great Britain, Germany, and France in 1910 had a combined mercantile steamship fleet of 1,965 iron-hull ships and 9,074 steel ones, all over 100 tons. (In the same year construction began on the 45,000 *Titanic*.) Much of that shipping was directed toward the Far East and its major port of Singapore, which was the location of W. Somerset Maugham's short story, "P & O," published in the 1920s. After describing the port, Maugham concludes:

> In the soft light of the evening the busy scene was strangely touched with mystery, and you felt that all those vessels, their activity for the moment suspended, waited for some event of a peculiar significance.

That event came little more than ten years later, on February 15, 1941, when approximately 70,000 British colonial troops surrendered the city to the Japanese. The invaders did not come from the sea but overland, down the Johore peninsula of Malaya. The city's fall may be said to mark the end of what the Indian historian K. M. Panikkar has called the "Vasco da Gama Epoch," the European maritime domination of Asia, begun when da Gama rounded the Cape of Good Hope and arrived in Calicut in 1498.

It also made transparent the new global age. Neither Europe nor its colonial empires, all "overseas," were henceforth of primary importance. In that mid-twentieth-century world so reproportioned by war, gunboat diplomacy, an old colonial tactic, seemed almost quaint in the face of the atomic bomb, a product lethally distributed from the air. The now outdated Eurocentric view of things was best considered a brazen attitude allowed by a time of simpler technologies and more numerous "great powers," all traditionally defined as European. However, the immediate effect of World War II was the take-off of the air age and the dominant presence of the Soviet Union and the United States in world affairs.

That the American navy by war's end was vastly larger than the Royal Navy, which had previously allowed Great Britain to "rule the waves," provides some indication of this global alteration. Perhaps more significant was the fact that sixty-six Japanese aircraft, some carrying bombs and others carrying torpedoes, flew in three waves over the British battleships *Prince of Wales* and *Repulse*, to sink them both on December 10, 1941, as they were returning from sea to Singapore where they had been sent to help reinforce the defense of that strategic port.

The fall of Singapore not only dramatically announced the end of dominant European seapower, it suggested the emergence of a new global geography in which contrails would replace the wake of ships as visible signs of human traffic. If further confirmation of this "sea change" of activity were needed, it was soon provided by the most significant of the events in the Pacific Theater of World War II. Between June 4 and June 7, 1942, the Battle of Midway took place. Urged on by the Japanese intention to conquer Midway Island, the battle involved two naval forces that never made contact by sea. It was on the wings of their planes, launched from aircraft carriers, that victory and defeat were carried forth. American carrier-based bombing planes sank four Japanese aircraft carriers, thereby crippling the Japanese navy. The American admiral in charge of the operation followed the activity by ear not by sight: he listened to radio reports; he did not stand on the bridge of his flagship with binoculars to his eyes.

Beyond this sea drama, enacted at frightful costs in lives, the Japanese made great headway on land in overrunning many of the European colonial possessions in the Far East. For a brief period of time, in 1942, Japanese armies even seemed poised to invade India. The rapidity of Japanese success was a measure of the tenuous nature of European colonial empire and seemed to offer confirmation of the argument that such empires were ridiculously overextended and had only been able to exist at a time when international relations were essentially defined as European relations, from which were generally absent, excluded, or dismissed the United States, Russia (before it was transmogrified into the Soviet Union), and Japan. The last, however, entered the European sphere when Great Britain signed an alliance with the Japanese in 1902 which guaranteed the status quo, an acceptance of each other's position in the Pacific Ocean.

World War II was the violent manifestation of globalization in which all the traditional "Great Powers of Europe" became secondary states. With this decline came two new conditions. First was the external overthrow of European colonial rule; second was the nearly vertical rise of the United States to great power status and the subsequent decline of Great Britain in particular, but of the other colonial powers as well, as they now came to depend on American arms and goodwill.

Exclusive of the European continental theater of warfare, which had soon become – since June 22 1941, the date Hitler invaded Russia – the stage of a titanic struggle between two land empires, those of Nazi Germany and the Soviet Union, the war elsewhere introduced a new phase in colonial history: vast military aggression. Until this time, colonial empire had been maintained "on the cheap," an activity that had not been heavy in the cost of lives of any of the participants, European or indigenous. Such a statement is not meant to imply that the military factor was insignificant, which indeed it was not, but that any battles were generally small in scale and short in duration: the terms "skirmish" and "foray" became popular descriptive terms. Now, however, warfare on a grand scale between equally well-equipped forces radically changed the colonial landscape. The Japanese overran most of the Southeast Asian colonies and many of the Pacific islands which also formed part of colonial empire. The fall of Corregidor, the military bastion of the Philippines, in May 1942, marked the momentary end of American power in the Pacific. Half a globe away, the Nazis overran much of North Africa in 1941–2 and briefly controlled Tunisia, Libya, and the western reaches of Egypt. This now famous "Desert War" was given its dimensions principally by Field Marshal Irwin Rommel who acquired a falsely romantic image as the "Desert Fox." However, in the celebrated Battle of El Alamein, on the threshold to the Suez Canal, the British, under the leadership of General Bernard Montgomery, turned the tide of battle, beginning on October 23, 1942, and finally forced the Germans and their Italian allies out of Egypt by November 12.

In the meantime, full-scale war erupted at the other end of North Africa, where, on November 9, the largest amphibious operation ever mounted until that time brought the Americans and British quickly in control of Algeria, a French colonial possession since 1830 when the French had mounted a much more modest naval bombardment and invasion. From there the Allies moved on to Tunisia, wresting it from the Germans in May 1943. Thus, North Africa became a major battlefield for outside contenders as it had not been since the time of the Fourth Punic War when the Romans sacked Carthage.

The year 1942 was when the war turned away from the imperialist advances of Nazi Germany and Imperial Japan. Although the war dragged on for another three years, its general movement was of slow retreat for Germany and Japan, slow advance for the Soviet Union, the United States, and Great Britain. The effective conclusion of the colonial aspects of that war was symbolically recorded on film as General Douglas MacArthur waded through the surf of the island of Luzon and thus gave visual validation to his famous remark, "I shall return," made as he had left Corregidor for Australia three years before.

In the agonizing interval the Japanese had established a hasty form of indirect rule in most of their captured territories whereby they removed the European colonial administrators and sought assistance from local leaders. In short time they had even allowed official independence: Burma on August 1, 1943; followed by the Philippines on October 14. Indonesia was about to be granted that status in August 1945, just as the Japanese war effort collapsed. Therefore, Sukarno personally took the initiative and officially established a republic on August 17, 1945.

Indochina was more complicated in its political play, as it would continue to be for another thirty years. The Japanese initially allowed the French administration to remain in place and maintained a minimal military force there for policing purposes. However, worsening relations between the two authorities intensified and, on March 9, 1945, the Japanese took direct control of the colony. They installed Bao Dai, the figurehead emperor of Annam under the French, who headed the independent state which he proclaimed on March 1, 1945. His office was a short-tenured one because he was ousted from power by supporters of Ho Chi Minh on August 25, 1945. Ho had founded the Vietminh, or National Front for the Independence of Vietnam, in 1941. Now he proclaimed the Democratic Republic of Vietnam on September 2, 1945, and prepared the way for nearly three decades of confrontation, first with the French and then with the Americans.

Somewhat removed from these major military and political developments was the island scene in which the Americans briefly pursued a form of military supply-base colonization, reluctantly permitted by the French. In the New Hebrides and on New Caledonia, as well as several other islands, large American bases were established. The story of their development is lyrically told in the American musical *South Pacific*, in turn a theatrical adaptation of the journalist James Michener's *Tales of the South Pacific*. Even more romantic in allusion, however, is the now famous "cargo cult," a hastily fabricated mythic tale by Pacific islanders of the Americans as White gods descending with hitherto unimaginable gifts, disgorged from landing ships. The myth would have it that these gods would return again, laden with commercially produced goodness.

What is significant from this small matter in the Pacific "theater of operations" is its place in the larger picture of decolonization. The wealth, organization, and power of the United States grandly over-shadowed whatever efforts the French had previously made as providers of economic betterment to their Pacific island colonies.

This activity, so discomforting to the colonial administrators but also so necessary to the war, must be considered in parallel with that gener-ated by the militarily aggressive Japanese. It is in a double sense – first, the dislodging of European colonial authority; and, second, the encour-agement of leaders protesting European domination – that the Japanese disturbed and weakened the colonial regimes, and thus contributed to the complicated set of occurrences grouped together as the process of decolonization. It is certainly true that the professed Japanese policy of "Asia for the Asiatics" was soon seen as only alliterative rhetoric for a new form of domination, but the opportunity to work against the former European colonial overlords was not ignored. That several of the prominent political figures in decolonizing Asia had served in major positions during the Japanese occupation is some indication of the effect Japan's own policy of imperialist expansion during the war had on the European colonial situation in the area. U Nu, foreign minister of Burma, later became prime minister of that country after it gained its independence from Great Britain; Sukarno became the first presi-dent of Indonesia after the Dutch left; and Manuel Roxas, a cabinet minister during the Japanese occupation, became the first president of the Philippines after it was granted independence by the United States.

The second conditioning factor of World War II on colonial affairs was the new global position assumed by the Americans. During World War II the United States rose to world dominance and therefore the anti-colonial attitudes of its leadership, both in the person of President Franklin D. Roosevelt and the officials in the Department of State, were very discomforting, particularly to the British. Colonial empire was seen by American officialdom rather in the way residents of Newark, New Jersey, viewed "The Empire," a downtown burlesque the-ater producing tawdry shows without merit in the interwar period. While suspicious of the entire colonial enterprise, Roosevelt was par-ticularly denunciatory of the French in Indochina. He argued that the Japanese gained control of that country quickly because the Indochinese, "so flagrantly downtrodden . . . thought to themselves: Anything must be better than to live under French colonial rule!"[1]

Opposition to traditional colonial rule was expressed in two ways in Washington. First, there was a desire for international trusteeship of the colonial territories; and, second, there was a policy statement on future independence. In between, however, were the unsettling demands of the American naval command which wanted to hold on to the Pacific islands conquered from the Japanese so that they might serve as permanent bases for future naval operations, if required. (The American base on Okinawa is a contemporary residual of that thinking.)

Early on in the war, in November 1942, the State Department issued an official paper, "Declaration of National Independence for Colonies," that urged acceptance of the principle of independence and requested that the colonial powers establish a timetable for such independence.[2] The British reaction, the only one so expressed because the other colonial powers were then defeated, was one of indignation and fear, leading to resistance. Some saw the American position as designed to assure American ascendancy in a postwar world; all concerned with the matter saw the American position as deleterious to British interests. Winston Churchill, then prime minister and ever an ardent imperialist, was the greatest defender of traditional British interests. Later he summed up his persistent attitude when he stated, in a discussion on the future of Hong Kong, "Hands off the British Empire is our maxim."[3]

During the war and shortly thereafter, the British were forced to tightrope walk between their own imperial interests, where they wanted freedom of action, and the exigencies of war, where the American alliance was essential. By 1944 when plans were being made for D-Day, the day of the naval invasion of German-held Europe, Great Britain seemed to have been reduced to a military staging area, no longer the seat of a colonial empire. The presence of 1.2 million American military personnel there in April 1944 is some sort of statistical confirmation of the shift in global power. To gain some perspective, consider that when Portugal began its overseas expansion in the fifteenth century and thus began modern European colonial empire, it had a national population roughly equalling the number of Americans in Great Britain just before D-Day.

Mass, in numbers of people assembled, goods produced, communications systems created – all these matters so grandly present on D-Day – indicated a new era in which small numbers of colonial administrators and small-scaled colonial budgets were reduced in consequence. The postwar world, as the French author Raymond Aron once remarked, was dominated by "continental monoliths." These were the United States and the Soviet Union. One note of confirmation of this new global expression of power: when Great Britain responded to the Falkland Island crisis of 1982 the government had to cancel the pending sale of the carrier HMS *Invincible* to Australia, which had already been designated by that nation's name, so that the vessel might comprise part of the required task force.

The very nature of World War II – defensive at best for the colonial powers – forced change. In 1942, with the threat of Japanese invasion of India, Winston Churchill sent Sir Stafford Cripps, a Labourite member of his wartime government, to India to negotiate. Cripps offered India dominion status after the war and the right to establish a constituent assembly, conditions tantamount to self-government but not yet outright independence. Negotiations were unsuccessful and were further aggravated by Mohandas Gandhi's newly pronounced "Quit India" position. Amidst violent protest, the British reinforced order, but only after having declared a new position from which they did not retreat. The issue was no longer one of continuing British control in whatever form but of complete departure in whatever way proved most feasible.

The French colonial position during the war was entirely different. The nation itself was cleft by the results of continental defeat at the hands of the Germans. Two governments then vied for control of the colonial empire. The Vichy regime, a puppet state which nominally ruled over two-thirds of France, established some control over most of the colonies by appointment of new officials loyal to it. The regime also exported its principles of National Revolution (*Partie, Famille, Travail* – or "Motherland, Family, Work" – was its motto) which led to racial segregation and severe labor impressment, conditions which starkly revealed the ugly side of French imperialism and generated further resentment to it.

From a short distance abroad, in London, General Charles de Gaulle, who established a Free French movement as a sort of government-in-exile, claimed control of the colonial territories. In his famous speech of June 18, 1940, broadcast shortly after he had arrived in the British capital from France, de Gaulle declared that "France is not alone! She has a great empire behind her." For de Gaulle, the colonial empire provided a territorial foundation for the government he headed in exile. After the invasion of North Africa in 1942, his government was installed there, thus suggesting a legitimacy which, however, was not recognized by the Americans until 1944. As many observers, then and later, have noted, President Roosevelt had no use whatsoever for General de Gaulle whose rhetoric and demeanor, like his stature (6 foot 4 inches), was lofty.

For de Gaulle the colonial empire was a source of France's greatness, a condition that he believed France had to maintain. This general assumption was reinforced at the Brazzaville Conference of 1944 which gathered administrators from all the French African colonies to discuss postwar policy, now that victory was certain. France's position, which was of course de Gaulle's, was straightforward and adamant, a reiteration of long-established colonial ideology: "The goals of the task of civilization accomplished by France in her colonies rule out any idea of autonomy, any possibility of evolution outside the French bloc of the empire." To assuage any opposition, de Gaulle encouraged the establishment of local representative bodies to assist in territorial governance.

Thus, as the war concluded in favor of the Allies, among whom were the two major European colonial powers, three distinct positions had been tentatively proposed for the colonial possessions: internationalization endorsed by the United States; devolution of some of the empire, notably India, by the British; retention of the structure of colonial empire with some slight modification by the French. As for the minor colonial powers, either occupied by the Germans – Holland and Belgium – or not directly involved in the war – Spain and Portugal – no change was envisioned, if considered at all, although the Dutch government-in-exile's wartime promise of independence to the Dutch East Indies was now conveniently forgotten.

Further complicating the colonial situation at war's end was the glaring display of the weakness of all the colonial powers, and this condition went beyond their dependency on the United States for military equipment and financial assistance. Only Great Britain at that moment retained any meaningful colonial authority and power. Therefore, the nation was called upon to assist in re-establishing a *pax colonia* of sorts in the ever-turbulent South Pacific region. As the Japanese military occupation of Southeast Asia ended, a power vacuum occurred. In the Dutch colonial territories, now known as Indonesia, and in French Indochina, national governments were quickly established with declarations of independence, as has been mentioned above. Before the Dutch and French could return in an effort to reassert their authority, the British Southeast Asia Command, under Lord Mountbatten, was designated to send in troops to maintain order. For nearly six months, the British did this in Indonesia and soon found themselves in a minor war with the nationalists. In Indochina the British occupied the lower half of the country, the area around Saigon, as Ho Chi Minh's Vietminh asserted its authority in the northern half of the country. The French arrived in the south in a matter of weeks and then took over from the British. Both instances clearly demonstrate the confused and unsettled condition of colonial empire in the

Pacific region at the end of the war. To this condition ought to be added the effects of the American fulfillment of a decade-old promise: the independence of the Philippines on July 4, 1946.

As victory in World War II drew in sight, American policy gained some resolution. However, this was not severely unfavorable to either Great Britain or France. At the Yalta Conference in February 1945, the principle of trusteeship was extended by the Americans only to the former mandate territories and the former colonies of Italy. In effect, British and French colonies were exempt, left to the particular conditions decided upon by these two nations. In the following year, when American foreign policy was becoming increasingly anti-communist because the national leadership was fearful of perceived Soviet expansionism, the value of the British empire as a bulwark against communism was beginning to be realized. Soon, on the occasion of the Korean War (1950–3), the French role in Indochina would be viewed that way as well. Here, in both instances, was expressed an ambiguous and seemingly inconsistent statement of American foreign policy: anti-colonial where the Russians did not appear as a threat, and supportive of the British and French position where their colonial activity could be trooped out as action against encroaching communism. The long involvement of the United States in Indochina/Vietnam is tragic proof of this ambivalence.

With the conclusion of a war so disastrous for all of the colonial powers, any notion of continuing policy and practice as before was discounted, de Gaulle's statements notwithstanding. No colonial power welcomed the thought of empire's dissolution, but all realized that some change was inevitable if a semblance of the old order was to be maintained. In a memorandum of 1942 an assistant under-secretary of the British Ministry of Colonies wrote: "Nineteenth-century conceptions of empire are dead."[4] As they attempted to resume their role in their colonial territories, almost all colonial nations recognized this fact. As they also soon learned, moreover, even major colonial reform promised no long lease on colonial rule.

The effect of war in the twentieth century on empire founded in the nineteenth has led to a lively historical debate. Viewed from the more narrow European perspective which seemed to go straight away from London or Paris to the colonies, only World War II was disastrous to empire. However, viewed globally, one can find signs of dissolution much earlier. The rapid success of the Americans in the Spanish–American War of 1898, that "splendid little war," proved that Spanish colonial rule had been at best a thin shell. The Russo-Japanese War of 1904–5, in which Russia was quickly defeated at sea, has long been considered a striking refutation of notions of "White supremacy" and European world domination. Certainly, that war removed any European doubts about the role Japan would play in the Pacific. Further proof of that island empire's oceanic ambition came with Japan's participation on the Allied side in World War I which allowed it to expand its empire at the expense of the German Pacific island possessions. Furthermore, American intervention in Mexico in 1914 and in Haiti in 1915 may be interpreted as a growing policy of American interventionism in those places that had once been colonized, a policy that would reach forward in time to the Gulf War of 1991.

World War I also added to the internationalization of colonial issues. The mandate system, put in place with the peace treaties, set a new tone, if not a new practice; and the existence of an international deliberative body in the form of the League of Nations can be seen, retrospectively, as a step toward the United Nations which would play a significant role in decolonization. The Soviet Union, born of the war, made the ideology of communism an article of exportation to the colonies where it mixed well with nationalism as a volatile combination of protest.

The broad significance of all of these considerations was anticipated early on, even before they gained their particular historical shape. In his popular text, *Imperialism and World Politics*, first published in 1926, Parker T. Moon, professor at Columbia University, stated: "Little as the general public may realize the fact, imperialism is the most impressive achievement and the most momentous world-problem of our age." Few supporters of empire at the time of that written assessment would have disagreed with the first part. The second part, however, only rang with truth after World War II.

3 Instability and uncertainty

The postwar situation

The historian's famous caution about *ex post facto* assessments should be borne in mind in any consideration of the rapid end of colonial empire. Because all of these European empires "fell" quickly, rather like houses of cards (but hardly in peaceful play), one can easily assume that the result was preordained or, at the very least, an expected outcome. Yet few individuals who supported empire thought that the game was up completely. In the immediate postwar environment of continental reconstruction and global realignment, colonial empire seemed chiefly to need its own "re" prefixed nouns: restoration of previous control and reform of previous policies. But the time for such efforts proved to be painfully short for those who believed in empire. Even before the fact of a "postcolonial world," a British critic wrote a widely read assessment of finality – John Strachey's *The End of Empire* (1959) – while an American academic wrote a widely used text as a sweeping analysis of decolonization – Rupert Emerson's *From Empire to Nation* (1960).

The very term "power" was one that the European nations could ill afford to use boldly after World War II as they had done before that war. These nations were all devastated by the war, with all but Great Britain defeated. With the exception of Italy which first lost its African empire to British forces early in the war and then found its homeland militarily occupied by the Germans who rushed in after the Anglo-American invasion of 1943, the others were under the Nazi boot through most of the war. The exceptions that prove the rule are Spain and Portugal, neither a "power" in the twentieth century, but both of which held on tenaciously to their scattered holdings. There is a sort of overarching historical irony in the fact that Portugal was both the first and the last European colonial nation, first picking up coastal territory in Africa in the late fifteenth century and only relinquishing its hold in 1975 when Mozambique, Guinea-Bissau, and Angola gained their independence.

None of this activity of political devolution was foreseen, let alone predetermined in 1945. The British, the most advanced and flexible in their thinking, were prepared to conclude the era of their rule in India, and likewise in Burma and Ceylon, as they did in 1947 and 1948, respectively. At the same time, they recognized their inability to hold on to Palestine, their situation there made impossible by Israeli terrorist tactics. The French, more adamant than the British in their will to hold on to the old way of things, had nonetheless conceded independence during World War II to their mandated territories, Syria and Lebanon, and did allow this change of status to occur in 1946. Despite its wartime-announced intention to grant independence, the Netherlands fought tenaciously from 1946 to 1948 to hold on to its multi-insular possession which was finally recognized as the Republic of Indonesia in 1949.

Yet those two nations with the greatest amount of foreign real estate tried immediately after the war to give to "empire" in name some of the structural unity it never had. As Europe repaired its domestic fortunes, its major colonial powers, Great Britain and France, sought to reassemble and redirect those colonies they still held into a loose whole, rather like a bunch of grapes. "Empire" and "colonialism" were excised from the official vocabulary. And the French, ever alert to the subtleties of language, substituted the title "resident" for "governor," a change suggesting a more neighborly arrangement of things.

For the British the "commonwealth" idea had emerged as an alternate arrangement to overbearing empire. Officially created at the Imperial Conference of 1926, the British Commonwealth of Nations was to consist of "autonomous communities within the British Empire, equal to each other" but with common allegiance to the Crown. Such an arrangement was made for the "White dominions," the former settlement colonies like Canada and Australia which had by the twentieth century both representative and responsible government. However, the many reforms for India initiated between the two World Wars moved the Commonwealth idea and organization forward and outward. When, after its independence in 1947, India was allowed to join the Commonwealth as a republic in 1949, it did so only with acceptance of the "King as the symbol of free association." Most of the emerging new nations of Africa that had gained independence from Great Britain joined the Commonwealth. This evolution, slow and uncertain, never truly calculated in advance, but generally responsive to changing conditions, gave to the decolonization of the British empire a smoother end or, perhaps better put, lessened the travail and turmoil that accompanied the French as they lost their colonial empire.

The French empire went through two transformations; a better term might be two public facelifts. The first occurred during the constitutional convention in 1946 when the Fourth Republic came into being. The new name for the French colonial empire became the "French Union," and its component parts, no longer colonies, were "associated states," and "associated territories" as well as "overseas departments." The new umbrella title and the territorial designations it covered did not entail any serious devolution of power. The French government still maintained control, and the President of the Republic was also President of the French Union. Later, after the Fourth Republic fell under the weight of the long and debilitating war fought to keep Algeria (1954–62), the new Fifth Republic reorganized what was left of the colonial empire into "the Community," a term somewhat harmonious with the British effort but unsupported by any reality. Created in 1958, the Community lost even its nominal existence in 1960. It was then that the member states in former French West Africa requested to exercise their option, guaranteed by the constitution of the Community, to become sovereign nations. In a matter of months they were all granted that independence. The exception, it should be noted, was French Guinea which had in 1958 exercised the most extreme choice offered at the inception of the Community. At that time, any colonial territory could choose to be integrated into France as a metropolitan department, could join the Community, or could elect independence, but this last option was to be accompanied by the immediate cessation of all French economic aid. When Guinea opted for independence, the French expressed the exactness of their intentions by taking as much equipment as they could when they departed, including telephones off the walls.

Much has been made of the different mind-sets and practices that informed both of these national attempts at the governance of colonial systems. The British had developed the notion of "trusteeship," particularly in the late nineteenth and early twentieth centuries, for those areas other than the self-governing colonies which were now described as dominions (Canada, Australia, and New Zealand being the chief ones). Trusteeship became very popular in the interwar era, as was described in the previous chapter, and provided both the concept and the means by which the British might depart from the colonial situation with some grace and some sense of self-fulfillment. The French, on the contrary, never completely abandoned their theory of "assimilation" and the centralization it provided. When, in the interwar period, the phrase "a nation of one hundred million" caught on, its appeal was expressive of the basic idea of assimilation, that France and the colonies, that Frenchmen and Africans, Asians, and Caribbeans formed some sort of whole, bound by a common culture and language which were both French, and by a continuing attitude expressive of the famous epigram of the Enlightenment figure the Marquis de Condorcet: "A good law is good for all peoples at all times." The conversion of this idea into a political tenet occurred at the Brazzaville Conference when the concluding document stated that any movement toward self-government "was to be avoided" because it was not needed.

There is no way, scientific or statistical, to measure the effect of these differing policies. But they certainly conditioned decolonization and made the experience easier for the British than for the French.

Both the Commonwealth of Nations and the Community were alike as new forms of spheres of influence. The "sterling zone," which the British wished to maintain to ensure some strong economic advantage by tying Commonwealth countries to the British financial system, was matched by the French who developed a CFA (French African Bank) franc zone in Africa under the financial control of the Bank of France. The British version collapsed more readily, both as a result of dreadful financial crises at home and the growing international trade domination of the United States. The French zone, smaller in scale and with much more limited foreign trade, lasted much longer, giving way only in 1996, with the CFA franc devalued by 50 per cent in Zaire (now the Democratic Republic of the Congo), where, however, the French assumed economic dominance – and even supplied military support for the new nationalist regime – after the Belgians had left in 1960.

All of this change and subsequent efforts by the European colonial theorists and practitioners, either to reconfigure European rule or to contain decolonization, were clear indications that the heyday of imperialism, of pomp and circumstance, was over.

The speed of the political change from colonial status to independence, from a few empires to many nations, was remarkable in Sub-Saharan Africa – between 1960 and 1963 almost all of colonial empire was swept away there – and has since become an interesting problem of historical analysis. The precipitous action of President Charles de Gaulle in 1960 was matched by a similar one undertaken by the Belgians who decided to abandon the Congo in the same year. The British, more given to slow devolution, found themselves with little choice but to follow. And so they did in Nigeria in 1960, Tanganyika in 1961, Uganda in 1962, Kenya in 1963, with Nyasaland (Malawi) and Northern Rhodesia (Zambia) in 1964. Southern Rhodesia added an embarrassing and agonizing condition to all of this, when its White settler regime unilaterally declared independence and established the last, if short-lived, "White settler" colony, finally becoming Zimbabwe in 1979.

It is always tempting to see chronological sequence as causality. Hence, in the history of decolonization, this "scram out of Africa" – the Kenyan politician Tom Mboya's phrase – can be seen not only as subsequent to but in part the result of the most commented on military debacle of the end of empire: the joint French–British invasion of the Suez Canal in 1956. Provoked by the nationalization of the canal by President Gamal Nasser of Egypt, and concerned by the rapidly changing disposition of power in the Middle East, the British and French decided to mount an aerial invasion, ostensibly to support the Israelis who were encouraged to invade Egypt. The purpose of the strategy was distinctly imperialistic: the overthrow of President Nasser.

While the plan was quickly a military success, with Egyptian troops thrown back, it was more dramatic as a diplomatic failure, an international embarrassment to both the British and the French. Seemingly contrived to occur just as the Americans were going to the polls to elect their president – who would again be Dwight D. Eisenhower – the plan was viewed as insulting as well as ill-timed. (That the forthcoming election did not enter the minds of any of the British or French planners only made the operation appear to be all the more careless.) The American response was thus structured as a reaction to what was considered old-fashioned imperialist politics. Eisenhower, through his secretary of state, John Foster Dulles, ordered Prime Minister Anthony Eden to withdraw troops immediately. From the other side of the Iron Curtain, the Soviet Union even threatened war. And in the United Nations, anger was at a high pitch with India roundly denouncing the invasion.

Nasser remained; the British and the French withdrew. The last brazen imperialist act in the manner of nineteenth-century European power politics was over. In retrospect the failed invasion urges the historical conclusion that this was the precipitant that brought colonial empire to an end. But such an interpretation asks too much. As humiliating as it was, as strongly opposed as it was by former colonial territories now sitting as sovereign nations in the General Assembly of the United Nations, the quickly aborted invasion only signaled the obsolescence of imperialistic tactics and the weakness of the two formerly great colonial powers in face of a new world of superpowers and international public opinion. But, as has been seen in this chapter, the French and British held on for several more years in Africa. More influential than Suez in 1956 was the Cold War that extended over a longer period of time and ranged farther in geographical effect.

The period of decolonization was the time of the *pax americana*, the latest in national efforts at international control and, clearly, the replacement of the preceding *pax britannia*. The development of an American global political view and comparable military commitment were features of a new foreign policy that grew out of World War II. Fighting on two major fronts that were not European – the North African and Pacific – the nation literally took a new stand on world affairs and soon assumed that peace could be best guaranteed by armed strength. President Franklin D. Roosevelt's America as the "arsenal of democracy" was also, under his successors, to be the vital defender of democracy against an expansionist and totalitarian Soviet Union and, soon thereafter, a "Red China." Determined to assure the United States and its way of life against any potential threats, postwar administrations made a blanketing ideology of anti-communism and a regular practice of military support to friendly nations the two principal elements of their foreign policy.

The Soviet Union loomed large and ominously in the eyes of American statesmen and military advisers. The bipolar world they now saw was as actively manufactured in Washington as it was in Moscow and certainly more so in its extension to the colonial regions. That the basic ideology of colonial liberation was a compound of nationalism and Marxism, with the second considered the more volatile element, led Americans to see the influence of the Soviet Union nearly everywhere. With the Cuban Missile Crisis of 1962, when the Soviets had set up missile sites directed against the United States, an anxious nation led by an anxious president, John F. Kennedy, sensed the imminence of war. Faced with a stern threat from the United States and a naval blockade of Cuba, the Soviets backed down, packed their equipment and went home. Yet Soviet interference in the former and remaining colonial world was growing.

It was in Africa that the chilling effect of the Cold War was most strongly felt. Newly freed African states and those struggling to create some semblance of political order were often caught up in Cold War rivalry. Certainly this was most obvious in the Belgian Congo where rival factions received rival support in a country which as a colony had been offered no preparation in the art of self-government. An effort to establish a break-away regime in the Katanga province, led by Moise Tshombe, was anointed by the Belgians; while the regime in Kinshasa (the former Leopoldville), under Patrice Lumumba, was sprinkled with the Soviet secular equivalent of holy water. Through United Nations intervention and American connivance, the matter was resolved, but not so happily. Lumumba was assassinated in 1961, and Tshombe was hastily ushered out of power. The American counter-intelligence agency, the CIA, saw in the person of a journalist named Joseph Mobutu a likely client and supported his brutal takeover of power in 1965. Restyled Mobutu Sese Seko, he stood against communism and allowed the gross exploitation of his nation's resources by foreign corporations; for which reason his own bank accounts rose as the nation's population sank into poverty.

There is no doubt that the Cold War complicated decolonization and that its effects disturbed the leaders of the new nations. As President Habib Bourguiba of the newly sovereign nation of Tunisia wrote in an article in the quasi-official American publication *Foreign Affairs* in 1957: "Neutralism in the cold war and neutrality in a 'hot' one are equally precarious." As for the United States, the Cold War made that nation something of a fitful arbiter of colonial affairs. The United States supported the continuation of European rule where it seemed to assure a bulwark against communism (as in Indochina after the outbreak of the Korean War in 1950), and it gave heavy military support to former colonial nations which seemed sturdy and determined enough to help stave off communism (of which American support to the regime of the Shah of Iran between 1953 and 1974 was the most notorious). The Soviets, having crushed opposition in their Eastern European empire, after running in tanks to put down Hungarian efforts at freedom in 1956 and thus securing their hold, were in a position to turn their attention to the former colonial world as well. Cuba and Ethiopia were the most obvious beneficiaries of Russian aid, but support to the liberation forces in Angola was also disconcerting to the United States and, in particular, its then secretary of state, Henry Kissinger. In many ways, some beneficial but most detrimental, the Cold War activities of the United States and the Soviet Union affected the course of decolonization, but they were in no way causal factors in its occurrence.

Viewing decolonization largely as an external matter, formed or generated, inspired or controlled from Whitehall, the Quai d'Orsay, or Foggy Bottom, respectively the particular locations of the British, French, and American foreign offices, the historian risks being in league with the earlier imperialists who established the idea of a Eurocentric world. The international policies of the Western nation states and the Soviet Union were, of course, significant matters, but they were not dominant factors.

Decolonization was a compound of individual national policy and of internationalism – this latter consisting of both political pressure, as exercised by the United States, and of international opinion and decision-making. And, most obviously, decolonization was also the result of the demand for reform, the protest against capricious colonial rule, and the struggle for independence – this last range of resentment reaching its extreme in the "national liberation movements." Decolonization might therefore be visually presented as an equilateral triangle, an arrangement of three parts of similar significance: national politics, international developments, and colonial protest movements.[1]

From the colonial condition of natives to the rebellious condition of nationalists, the leaders and their followers in Africa and Asia after World War II variously sought accommodation and freedom from the Europeans.

Greeting the Dutch when they returned to Jakarta and other Indonesian cities was, among other unpleasant matters, graffiti. "Indonesia for Indonesians" said a popular slogan – and in English. By the time such words as these were inscribed on the walls of buildings, the Vietminh had already pulled down the statue of Paul Bert, a former French colonial administrator, from the central position it occupied in Hanoi.

The signs of the times no longer favored the Europeans.

4 Pronouncements, denunciations, and the search for ideology
International public opinion and decolonization

If the hard material of revolution is steel, the stuff of protest is words: words constructed into declarations, manifestos, pronouncements; words selected to reconfigure the present and to shape the future. Just as the Enlightenment of the eighteenth century was a literary dissent from the old order of things, so decolonization was also a literary movement that vigorously protested the imperial order of things. Therefore, decolonization may be considered as much a verbal contest as it was a set of physical confrontations, its setting as frequently the conference hall in a major city as the battleground in the countryside.

The leaders of the reform and protest movements in the colonial world formed part of an intellectual elite. Frequently educated in European and American universities, skilled in the use of the European languages that provided access to a wide readership, knowledgeable of the European philosophical tradition of protest, and often writing and organizing their initial efforts in the capitals or major cities of the countries whose colonial policies they roundly denounced, these individuals adapted and reworked European thought to express their own concerns and intentions.

Their articles and books were many, varying in tone from elegiac considerations of the spirit of a people to strident denunciations of European civilization. In the first category was the idea of *négritude*, expressive of the spirit and sensibility of the Black man which Leopold Sedar Senghor, poet, philosopher, and soon to be president of Senegal, described romantically in 1956 in an article entitled "African-Negro Aesthetics" which appeared in the American publication *Diogenes*: "He [the Black] is first of all sounds, odors, rhythms, forms and colors; I mean that he is touch before he is sight, unlike the White European." In the second category was the Martiniquan poet Aimé Césaire's *Discourse on Colonialism* (1972) in which he sharply argued that Adolf Hitler had "applied to Europe colonialist procedures," that Hitler's practices and those of colonialism were as one: the humiliation and degradation of the human being.

The extensive body of literature, of which the above selections were a part, was directed principally not to the oppressed but to the declared oppressor, to those Europeans and Americans who experienced empire only as a subject of study and who might accordingly be persuaded of its harmfulness. "Europeans, you must read this book and enter into it," advised and warned the French existentialist philosopher Jean-Paul Sartre in the preface to arguably the most powerful and influential work of protest, Frantz Fanon's *Wretched of the Earth*, first published in French by a Parisian publishing house in 1961 and subsequently translated into English and published in the United States. A review of one of the later editions in *Time* magazine (April 30, 1965) stated: "This is not so much a book as a rock thrown against the window of the West." The analogy was appropriate because Fanon's central thesis was that colonization had been a violent act and could only be removed, thrust out, by violence. Decolonization, he said "evokes for us the searing bullets and bloodstained knives which emanate from it." It is the brutal means by which the last shall be first, he contended.

Few books about decolonization have received as much attention or generated as much controversy as this one. In the ten years from its first publication in 1961, it was reprinted eight times in France, was printed four times in the United States and three times in Great Britain. (It was not printed in Algeria, its particular subject and setting, until 1987, twenty-five years after that country's independence – an interesting fact of the postcolonial era.) The book, therefore, stands as an obvious proof of the importance of a new international phenomenon, only widespread after World War II: the existence of an international public opinion which, through the use of polls, could be ascertained with some degree of accuracy and which, accordingly, commanded attention and aroused response.

The pace of decolonization, in the main concluded in twenty-five years, was in some measure a function of a time of rapid communications in which words and images reached far and arrived swiftly, "impacting," in our current idiom, a large audience. In this era newspapers and journals proliferated, radios and movie houses became commonplace in the colonial world, both reinforcing and expanding the activities of the colonial intellectual elite and generating a public awareness, through spoken word and image, among the vast, still illiterate populations. The movie, as both a means of mass entertainment and mass information, early on played an influential role. Social criticism had become something of a hallmark in the Tamil-language films that were produced in Madras, one of India's film centers between the wars.

Figures like Jawaharlal Nehru and Kwame Nkrumah gained international recognition as their photographs joined those of Western leaders in the galleries of widely circulated magazines. (For example, in 1946–7 seven photographic portraits of Nehru appeared in major American publications, six in British; and in 1957 seven portraits of Nkrumah appeared in major American publications.) The newsreel, a feature of movie theater offerings in the 1930s, had brought Mohandas Gandhi before the eyes of millions, his diminutive, scantily clad figure serving as a stunning contrast to the power and trappings of the British Raj it defied, and also appearing as a simple and stark statement of righteousness. In 1954, the year of their victory over the French in a well-executed siege against the fortified outpost the French had set up at Dien Bien Phu, the Vietnamese released a major documentary film bearing the name of the battle as its title. In 1970 a newly formed group from the former French possessions of Africa, the Pan-African Federation of Film Makers (FEPACI or the Fédération Panafricaine des Cinéastes), issued a statement of purpose which emphasized the need for film makers to assist in the cultural liberation of Africa. Reflecting on that early need, the Senegalese film maker Ousmane Sembene commented in 1978: "For us, African film makers, it was then necessary to become political, to be involved in a struggle against . . . all the things that we have inherited from the colonial and neo-colonial systems."[1]

Whether composed by creative writer, artist, or politician, the resulting body of work was, as had been European nationalist ideology a century before, forward-looking but historically conscious. An imagined precolonial past would give direction to an imagined postcolonial future. The colonial present, like a parenthesis, would only briefly block narrative continuity. Nehru had long written of the length and grandeur of Indian history. African authors were doing likewise. Cheikh Anta Diop of Senegal, the most famous, persuasive, and controversial of them all, looked far back to see that the achievements of Pharaonic Egypt were essentially those of a negroid people and, consequently, to conclude that Western civilization had Black African origins. "Henceforth," he therefore asserted, in his very controversial study, *Nations negres et culture* (1954), "the Black must be capable of recovering the continuity of his national past." In the first years of the existence of the Republic of Ghana, postcards appeared showing Black Africans as tutors of historic figures familiar to Europeans as the architects of the "classical age."

The outpouring of such arguments and sentiments was extensive in fact, if not greatly varied in form. If it represented a new spirit of self-assertion, it was also directed against a domineering Europe. First, in rhetorical consideration, therefore, was imperialism, invariably described as abusive, oppressive, and destructive. It was now seen, if not so vividly described, as Joseph Conrad had written of it a half-century before in *Heart of Darkness* as "a flabby, pretending, weak-eyed devil of a rapacious and pitiless folly." It was the perceived weakness and indecisiveness of the imperialist powers that strengthened the arguments and intensified the protests of the colonial opposition. Second in rhetorical consideration was national affirmation, perhaps best expressed by Amilcar Cabral, leader of the revolutionary movement in Guinea-Bissau in West Africa, who argued in a speech given before an American university audience in 1970 that the right of each people was both to its destiny and to its own history, the latter having been "usurped by imperialism." Third in rhetorical consideration was economic well-being, economic development, what would soon be called in academic parlance "modernization." Few were the opposition leaders who, like Gandhi, looked forward by fondly regarding a simpler past when spinning wheels, not steel rolling plants, dotted the countryside. Largely socialist in tone and intention, the rhetoric of protest embraced Western concepts of economic growth while also denouncing class exploitation. The Marxist dichotomy of exploiting capitalist and exploited proletariat was simply enlarged and internationalized to become exploiting colonial nation and exploited colonial people.

Eventually, these thoughts, spoken or written, were gathered together in collections and published. Nehru's works, even in selected form, comprise seventeen volumes and occupy three feet of library shelf space. Exceptional only in quantity, this publication was commonplace in purpose: historic justification, a further accounting to world opinion. Perhaps the most interesting of all such efforts to assure a favorable light on the personal role of the opposition leader in decolonization was the autobiography, the literary genre of self-affirmation. The now familiar historical figures of Gandhi, Nehru, and Sukarno, and lesser ones like Patrice Lumumba of the Republic of the Congo, so summarized themselves in print; and so has Nelson Mandela. These volumes were explanations and justifications of the role played by their authors in the political evolution of their own country, and the autobiographies indirectly signal the importance of the charismatic figure in modern state development in the colonial world where national institutions were few and loyalties divided. Kwame Nkrumah, first prime minister and then president of Ghana, produced a work with the title *Ghana, The Autobiography of Kwame Nkrumah* which was published, appropriately enough, in 1957, the year of Ghana's independence. Later, Nkrumah would be denounced for developing a "cult of personality," but the title of his autobiography is only exaggerated, not totally incorrect.

It was, however, the collective expression of written protest that was the most formative. In the form of manifestos, resolutions, declarations, and principles, Africans and Asians placed their case before the "court of world opinion." Nehru, in a speech to the Indian National Congress in 1929, said, "I appeal to Parliament and to the conscience of the world" to respond to India's forced subordinate political position. Collective expressions of such discontent were numerous in the early twentieth century. The first of the many Pan-African Conferences was held in London in 1900; a major international meeting, the International Conference Against Imperialism and Colonial Oppression, was held in Brussels in 1927 and was attended by Nehru and Senghor, among others. In New York City in 1943 a Nigerian graduate student at Columbia University, K. O. Mbadiwe, founded the African Academy of Arts and Research which held lectures, published papers and sent its own observer to the San Francisco United Nations Conference in 1945 where he issued a memorandum asking that the new international body recommend that the colonial powers establish a timetable for freedom of their colonies.[2] Several African groups then headquartered in London, the best known of which was the West African Students Union, had jointly submitted a manifesto with a similar request to the United Nations in April 1945.

In the final years of imperialism, a number of international conferences was held, often seen by their initiators as complementary to the activities of the United Nations and often expressive of the ideals that circulated rhetorically in the halls of the UN Building in New York. In a sense an articulate community of the oppressed developed in these years. What no one initially expected and what everyone now knows is this: the United Nations became the major international forum in which the smaller and middle-sized nations fighting the gravitational pull of the United States and the Soviet Union (the so-called bipolarization of the world) could present their views and influence world events. Initially consisting of 51 nations, among which only 4 had been of recent colonial status, the United Nations saw its roster grow to 122 by 1967, at which time 49 former colonies, now states, had joined. The critical weight of this number was significant. In 1961, for instance, a resolution calling for immediate decolonization of the remaining territories of the world was submitted by 26 Asian and African countries and supported by a total of 89 representatives so as to win heavily. Perhaps more impressive was the 1973 resolution introduced by 65 states and voted upon favorably by 92 that denounced Portugal's "illegal occupation of the republic of Guinea-Bissau," a territory that the Portuguese considered an integral part of their nation. Finally, the election of U Thant of Burma as Secretary-General of the United Nations in 1962 is further indication of the critical weight the former colonial territories were exercising as sovereign states in this world body.

In the deliberations of the nearly two dozen major regional and international conferences held around the world at this time, four principal concerns were regularly expressed: first, the elimination of colonialism and imperialism; second, economic development; third, respect for individual state sovereignty; fourth, the establishment of a peaceful world order in which the powerful nations would respect the small and middle-sized ones. Beginning with the third Pan-African Conference, held in Manchester, England, in 1945, these conferences internationalized the colonial question and soon assured that imperialism would bear only one connotation, that of oppression. By the 1970s the idea of "two imperialisms," those of the United States and the Soviet Union, was being heatedly discussed, while the idea of a "Third World" found between the two superpowers was widely accepted.

If such attitudinal change had a particular event as its beginning, that was the convening of the international conference in the Indonesian city of Bandung in 1955. This conference was first distinguished by its geographical range, with delegates coming from twenty-nine states in Asia and Africa representing about 56 per cent of the world's population. President Sukarno said in his address of greeting that "we are united by a common detestation of colonialism, in whatever form it appears." The subsequent Bandung Declaration upheld the principles of national sovereignty, respect for human rights, and equality among nations and peoples.

Of global proportions as no other such conference before had been, and a conference of states with ministerial representation as had been no other, Bandung took place at a time when the Cold War had reached beyond the confines of Europe and the Middle East to take on global proportions. The United States, pursuing a policy of containment, had entered the Korean War in 1950 and had supported the French with military equipment in Indochina at the same time. The conferees at Bandung, where Communist China played a significant role, sought a course between the two superpowers, the United States and the Soviet Union.

The notion of a "Third World," a reordering of international politics by new divisions, emerged from this conference. This new triangulation was a simple geometry of protest against the East–West division of a capitalist world and a communist world, the one having its magnetic pole in Washington, the other in Moscow, hence the popular term "bipolarization." As they moved from colonial status to the condition of nation states, the smaller and middle-size countries desired to avoid overbearing alliances and alignments. Habib Bourguiba, president of Tunisia, wrote in his article of 1957 of his fellow countrymen, "They do not wish to be drawn into armed conflict nor to find their country once more a battle-field over issues which chiefly concern the Great Powers."

Originally including states that had recently felt the effects of imperialism either directly or indirectly – hence the appearance of China at the Bandung Conference – the Third World later expanded to include Latin America which had ended its colonial condition a century and a half before and which was now seen as a continuing victim of economic imperialism, notably that indirectly exercised by North American corporations.

International politics was sharply triangulated. In this new scheme, the world was made up of a large base of "underdeveloped" nations with a huge concentration of population over which was a divided apex made up of the "developed" (highly industrial) nations either siding with the United States or the Soviet Union.

The event that marked this change in political geography was the first Conference of Non-Aligned Countries that met in Belgrade, Yugoslavia, and not in a colonial city, in 1961, one year after most of the French and British West African colonies had gained their independence. Building upon the precedent of Bandung, five national leaders – Nehru of India; Sukarno of Indonesia; Nkrumah of Ghana; Gamal Nasser, president of the new United Arab Republic; and Tito (Josip Broz), president of Yugoslavia – issued invitations to the conference that had the expressed intention of keeping clear of the chilling effects of the Cold War. Twenty-five states attended the conference and were, most significantly, joined by representatives from nineteen liberation movements. The Final Declaration of the conference called for peaceful coexistence, reduction of East–West tension, and respect for the independence and integrity of all states. Fourteen of the twenty-seven items in that declaration were directed against imperialism and colonialism.[3] Seven further conferences of non-aligned nations followed, down to 1986, with participating nations at the last conference numbering one hundred.

The significance of these international conferences on decolonization is difficult to ascertain, easy to ignore. Few scholars now pay much heed to them because they were not instrumental to change. They did, however, provide a forum at which grievances could be loudly expressed; they did serve to generate a community of common interests. And they did inform their participants, coming from diverse parts of the world, that imperialism was their common problem. "Our presence," said Amilcar Cabral at the first Tricontinental Conference held in Havana in 1966, "is in itself a cry of condemnation of imperialism and a proof of solidarity with all peoples who want to banish from their countries the imperialist yoke."

If the underlying premise and the binding factor of all these international conferences was negative – anti-imperialism – each also announced a cooperative spirit and searched for a transcendent ideology that would unify. The two predominant ideologies were Pan-Africanism and neutralism.

Pan-Africanism reaches back to the nineteenth century when Caribbean authors spoke of the common origins and common plight of Blacks on both sides of the Atlantic. In the early twentieth century, however, the movement gained both form and direction primarily from the energetic leadership of the American scholar and critic W. E. B. DuBois. It was he who organized what was labeled and was in fact the first Pan-African Conference in Paris on the occasion of the peace negotiations following World War I. Fifty-seven representatives from the Caribbean, the United States, and Africa attended and discussed broad issues, such as political reform – but no discussion of independence – and economic development that were designed to benefit Africans, and Black people throughout the world.

Directed and dominated by African-Americans, this conference was exceeded in importance by the fifth Pan-African Conference held in Manchester in 1945, the one in which Africans, notably Nkrumah and Jomo Kenyatta of Kenya, played significant roles. The management and direction of the conference were primarily African rather than African-American. The chief demand set forth by the conferees was African independence. However, there was also expressed a strong interest in framing that independence within a West African federation.

The 1956 conference pointed up the underlying difficulties in the ideology of Pan-Africanism. A response to White racism and the condition it imposed on Blacks everywhere, Pan-Africanism was first and foremost a movement of redress of these socio-economic abuses Blacks suffered. There was also talk of unification, of bringing the disparate colonies in Africa together into some kind of federal state. No one at this time was quite so bold as Marcus Garvey, the Jamaican who led the "Back to Africa" movement in the 1920s and declared himself president of the United States of Africa. The federal principle quickly waned,

however, as men like Nkrumah and Kenyatta returned to their home-
lands and fought distinct battles against the colonial status of these
separate places and, in the course of events, became heads of state not
willing to relinquish the power they had fought to obtain.

In the academic discussion of Pan-Africanism, the ideology has been
treated as political, economic, and cultural. Independence, economic
development and the search for what was defined as the "African personality" were all proposed and discussed. However, the Manchester
Pan-African Conference was the last to bear that name and no other
broad meeting of African peoples took place until 1958 when Nkrumah
hosted the All-African People's Conference, by which time he was head
of state in Ghana.

Neutralism fared little better. As the ideology of non-alignment, it
fostered a spirit of international cooperation among Third World
nations and emphasized its opposition to power politics and to international conflict. It also officially played down nationalism as a
disruptive and divisive force by interpreting it as a means to cooperation
and mutual support. The nation state was seen as the protector of culture and the opponent of cultural imperialism, but it was also
considered the basis of "collective self-reliance." This latter notion
emerged at the fourth Conference of Non-Aligned Countries held in
Algiers in 1973. Adopting an "Action Programme for Economic
Cooperation," the delegates supported the idea of a new economic
order in which participating states would provide support to those less
"developed" and needful of economic support.

Later critics would argue that the notion of "development" became
as Eurocentric as had been imperialism, that the Western model was
adapted to conditions unfavorable to its success. The number of international airports that altered the former colonial landscape and the
number of new national airlines that flew in and out of these airports
comprised only one such proof. World renowned critics, like the
Swedish author Gunnar Myrdal, complained of the decolonized
world's false start: the effort to build an industrial economy where a significant agrarian base had not yet been established. Expressions of
concern over the need for a "green revolution" were published in considerable numbers in the 1970s.

The conclusion to be drawn from an examination of this intense and
widespread expression of dissatisfaction is the obvious one: words of
protest in the 1950s and 1960s were strong, widespread, and of considerable impact. They comprised much of the force that led Prime
Minister Harold Macmillan to acknowledge the presence of the "wind
of change" in a speech he gave in Cape Town, South Africa, in 1960.

Figure 1   The British Empire Exhibition of 1924 shown at night. (*Illustrated London News*)

Moments of light   A high moment in the history of empire and a final one in decolonization; both these events were brightly and proudly illuminated.

Figure 2   The grand fireworks display over Victoria Harbour, Hong Kong, on the night of the final hand-over of the territory to China, June 30, 1997 (*Los Angeles Times*, photo: Steve Stroud)

Figure 3 "The most successful ceremonial fiasco in history" (Mountbatten). Lord and Lady Mountbatten drive in traditional fashion through central Delhi on the day the British Raj ended, August 15, 1947. Unable to find his car, Pandit Nehru is seen riding on the canopy, and in the rear of the landau sit three women and a child whom Mountbatten invited aboard so that they might escape the press of people. (*Illustrated London News*)

The ceremonial and the combative   Two aspects of decolonization

Figure 4   A French armored patrol seeking out National Liberation Front guerrillas in the Algerian desert, 1955 (*Illustrated London News*)

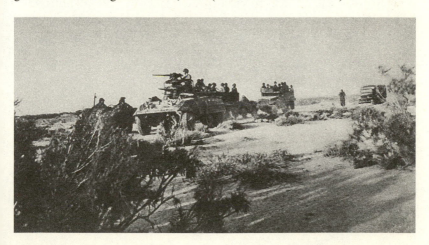

5 Countryside and city
The two landscapes of decolonization

The classic division of modern human activity into two distinct ecologies, that of countryside and that of city, was a pronounced condition in the colonial world of the twentieth century and served both to heighten and to complicate decolonization. Even though European influence was concentrated in the cities, it spread across the countryside as well and thereby affected each ecology significantly, but in distinctive ways.

The point is this: the Europeans did not like the land the way it was. Their intention was always alteration; their vision was always of a new environment largely shaped to provide local approximations of what ideally had existed or did exist at home. For some colonial administrators that vision was feudal, of a baronial agrarian system with the European administrator standing in as lord of the manor, overseeing the work of the peasants while providing them with order and peace. For others, that vision was more modern, a scene of neat farmsteads, sweeping plantations, well-ordered cities – all productive, all profitable. In fact, however, local ecologies were intruded upon and altered in a manner more haphazard than calculated, more brutal than considerate, more with the intention of securing immediate economic advantage and effective political control than with concern for the future welfare of the resident population.

This set of incongruities derived directly from the unique nature of the colonial system in the early twentieth-century world. In contrast with a Europe of political leaders and parties, of entrepreneurs and corporations, the colonies were directed by the colonial administrator and his staff, who dictated more than they negotiated, who saw themselves as rulers and constructors, those who ordered and arranged. They were the "cultural brokers" who attempted to turn what existed to their advantage and to change what seemed inappropriate or unsatisfactory.[1] Dominate in order to serve; such was the title of a volume (*Dominer pour servir*) written in 1946 by the governor of the Belgian Congo, Pierre Ryckmans. It may not be surprising to note that the most popular of British-produced movies about empire in the interwar years, *Sanders of the River*, released in 1936, was derived from the stories of that name which had been largely written by Edgar Wallace before World War I. Sanders, with pipe in one hand and walking stick in the other, wields feudal authority or, perhaps more appropriately, assumes a geographically misplaced role as one of the country gentry of the eighteenth century. In one scene in the film Sanders stands before a seemingly surly "native" and confronts him directly by pointing his stick at the African's chest. The "bit" player who received that small tip of attention was Jomo Kenyatta, later the first president of Kenya.[2]

In the cities the scene was not the same as in the countryside. In the larger and older ones, and also ones in which a considerable European population resided, power and authority were shared by the administrators, the professionals, and the merchants. If more obvious in the cities than in the countryside, the economic activities in the colonies were European by definition and market driven in purpose. No one can deny that whatever its particular cause or justification, the individual colonial territory was intended to be economically viable, not only to pay its own keep but to turn some sort of profit. Therefore, the configurations of the land were redrawn to serve purposes largely external to those of the local populations.

None of this was new, of course. European economic penetration of other continents began early with the spice, silk, and slave trades, with the ages-old search for gold and the newer one for exotic products like sugar and tobacco. The industrialization and embourgeoisement of Europe intensified and, accordingly, diversified colonial economics that emerged in the nineteenth century. Ivory for piano keys, ladies' combs and knick-knacks on mantelpieces; rubber for factory belts and automobile tires; diamonds for engagement rings and industrial cutting tools; bananas, coconuts, and pineapples to enrich the table; such were the most obvious of products cultivated or exploited in the colonial world.

New plantations grew. Nothing was more impressive in production and more oppressive to the local population than the rubber plantations of Indochina, dominated by the Michelin tire company. Rubber had only been introduced into Indochina in 1897, but within thirty years some 127,000 hectares (approximately 318,000 acres) of land were devoted to the crop. In Africa Lord Delamere, the most famous of the British aristocrats in Kenya, controlled over 100,000 acres of land on which he raised cattle and sheep. Some of the people under colonial rule also attempted to profit from the imposed system, turning to cash crops and to European utensils (plows, for instance) to ensure their success. But their efforts were hampered by colonial policies whereby Europeans gained access to good land and the indigenous population was, accordingly, displaced. In *The Wretched of the Earth* Frantz Fanon, the severe critic of European colonialism, said it was the settler who was the enemy. And it was in settlement colonies, Algeria the most obvious, but Kenya, Southern Rhodesia, Angola, and Mozambique as well, where decolonization was the most brutal.

As recent anthropological studies have shown, colonial policies given to economic development disrupted the local sense of place and space. Previously established networks of people, reinforced by long-cherished concepts of the purpose of the land, were distended, made larger in a way unpleasant and confounding to the indigenous population. Chinua Achebe, in the first of his now famous three novels on the effect of such change in Nigeria, describes it well. His hero, who initially succeeds by following older notions of manhood and manly activity, is caught up in change that he neither understands nor can effectively relate to. He is, as the title of the book, first published in 1958, suggests, living in a world where "things fall apart," the famous line of William Butler Yeats.

Cities, old and universal institutions, appeared in new form and in places suitable to European economic interests in the colonial environment. Nairobi in Kenya began in the early twentieth century as a railhead; Casablanca grew at the same time from a small fishing village to a major North African port. Before them, Singapore and Hong Kong were British creations, as were St Louis and Dakar French creations in Senegal. The rapid urbanization of the colonial world in the twentieth century was a major development of European-imposed intentions and demands.

With these changes came significant demographic ones as well. The colonial situation encouraged immigration: Chinese came to Malaya to work the tin mines; Indians arrived in East Africa to build the railroads; Lebanese arrived in West Africa to serve new commercial needs, particularly as shopkeepers. Asians and Africans moved about in their own lands, most particularly as they went to the cities to seek work or, as in the obvious instance of South Africa, to work the gold and diamond mines.

This brief overview suggests something of the distinctiveness of the countryside–city dichotomy in the colonial world. There was a peculiar and disruptive dynamic about it, as the various groups attempted to adjust to and profit from the new conditions. Granted a large portion of the indigenous population hewed to old ways, the capitalist system with its market economy greatly and gravely influenced the local ecologies. Decolonization, so regularly interpreted as a set of political problems involving local nationalisms and international relations, was also rooted in the countryside and grounded in the city. The ecology of the matter therefore merits being given some attention.

Dislocation and growth, those characteristics of "modernization" which usually meant movement from countryside to city and the appearance of new urban forms, were the two principal features of what might be described as the landscape of discontent. Particular grievances were generated by these new conditions. The loss of land and the implementation of taxes in the countryside, and unemployment and discriminatory residential zoning in the city were the most obvious. What was called "nationalism" in the colonial world was a political compound of localized protest and overarching ideology. The shrewd, as well as inspired, opposition leaders recognized the need to gain the support of the peasant as well as that of the city dweller. Colonial "nationalism" was therefore an expression of a dual focused rhetoric directed by an urban elite primarily to the Europeans whom they opposed, and secondarily to the local peasantry whose support they needed. The despoilers were the one; the disinherited were the other. As many critics have said, no successful protest movement was made without ideology and without peasant support. "National liberation" was more euphemism than expression of existing conditions. Many of the colonies had no preceding national history. Algeria and Nigeria, for instance, were strictly colonial administrative conveniences. And even modern India, as a state, received its boundaries as a result of British aggression and negotiation. When Kwame Nkrumah selected the name "Ghana" for the former colony of the Gold Coast, he reached back in time to the medieval African empire of Ghana, of which the territory of the Gold Coast had not been a part. As if according respect to the imperialist dividers of Africa, the delegates to the first meeting of the Organization of African Unity in Addis Ababa, May 1963 agreed to maintain the territorial boundaries defined at the Berlin West African Conference of 1884–5.

The problem of "national liberation" throughout most of the colonial world was less the need to recover a past than to convert the present political condition: the need to establish within the former colonial framework a nation. To use an old European metaphor, it was a matter of putting new wine in old bottles. The intellectuals, who considered the need, and the peasantry, which felt it, were joined together, each for different but complementary reasons, in fostering nationhood.

Of all the statements made by the opposition leadership in the time of decolonization, none more clearly or succinctly discussed this relationship than that made by Amilcar Cabral in a lecture he gave in 1970 at Syracuse University – and therefore to an American academic audience geographically and culturally removed from the world he described. Cabral revised the Marxist dialectic of class struggle to suggest the need of a symbiotic relationship which brought together the two distinct socio-economic groups engaged in the struggle for national liberation. The leaders, primarily issuing from the urban bourgeoisie, "discover at the grass roots the richness of their cultural values," while the peasants now "in contact with other groups . . . break the bonds of the village universe to integrate progressively into the country and the world." The provincial deeply enriches; the urban widely opens out. The two groups thus create a sense of national consciousness. In effect, what Cabral argued was not very different from nineteenth-century European notions of the relationship between folk wisdom and schooled intelligence. What distinguished colonial nationalism from European nationalism of the previous century was the more active role played by those living in the countryside; they needed little convincing.

The environment in which national liberation movements were fostered, the city, was also the place of European colonial concentration. The largest portion of the European population resided there; the major garrisons were there; the communications centers were there; the best of amenities (paved roads and covered sewers, race tracks, and clubs) were there. There, also, the indigenous population lived in an alien and isolated condition.

Most colonial cities were "two towns": the result of racial discrimination. There were "reserved" areas, where under the guise of sanitation, medical necessity, or professed concern with the retention of "native ways," the African and the Asian were restricted from residence and tolerated only as servants. With this condition came a stark imbalance in land use. The example of Nairobi is one of the most telling: in 1912 the 2,325 Europeans living in that town did so comfortably on 2,700 acres of land, while some 4,300 non-Europeans, principally Indian, lived in the bazaar which encompassed only 7 acres of land. No more apt description of this general condition of two distinct living environments so closely aligned can be found than that expressed by Obi Okonkwo, the hero of Chinua Achebe's novel *No Longer at Ease* (1960). Regarding both parts of Lagos, Nigeria, he was reminded "of twin kernels separated by a thin wall in a palm-nut shell. Sometimes one kernel was shiny black and alive, the other powdery white and dead."

Nowhere did such sharp division of residential zones match that maintained in South Africa. From the introduction of the term "location" as one of spatial discrimination in the nineteenth century until the establishment of apartheid as official policy in 1948, the White government of South Africa understood the significance of geography as a means of political control. Pass laws controlled the access that Black Africans had to White enclaves, and the state, in imitation of the private practice in the Kimberley mining compounds, built "native" housing, as in Durban, so as to control patterns of residence and to ensure the ability to police them. It is not overstating to say that urban policy was police policy, in turn state policy of the government in what was first the British Dominion of South Africa and then, after 1961, the Republic of South Africa.[3] And, conversely, the recent urban crisis from the 1970s onward can "be seen as the centre of the crisis of apartheid."[4]

In few other places was the urban crisis of such direct consequence. Yet, the declining years of colonialism were the very ones in which the problems of urban concentration rose. If urbanization is the most striking global phenomenon of the twentieth century, as it has been argued, such growth was more boldly marked in the colonial environment than it was in the European. In terms of demographic statistics, the growth was spectacular. For instance, Dakar, in Senegal, grew from a population of 1,600 in 1878 to one of 214,000 in 1955; while Hong Kong grew from a population of 160,402 in 1881 to one of 2,360,000 in 1950. Moreover, the ethnic disparity – the ratio of Europeans to others – was incomparable to that found in any part of the Western world. Everywhere, the European was a distinct minority. Even in Algeria, the one French settlement colony of the era of modern imperialism, about 70 per cent of the 820,000 Europeans in 1920 was urban, among a total population of some 8 million. By the 1950s 875,000 of the European population of about 1 million were resident in the cities.

While the full measure of this erratic urban development is difficult to determine, it was of such a scope as to create discontent with the order of things and to generate the hope of change promised by the new protest leaders. These individuals also benefited from another change which was urban sited.

As the purpose of the colonial enterprise went from domination to development, political reform occurred. What the Europeans now realized was the need to enlist the new elites, both professional and commercial, in achieving the economic growth that they considered necessary to revitalize their national economies after World War II. The British government's allocation of £120 million in 1944 – a war

year, of course – as support for a Colonial Development and Welfare
Act was motivated by a desire to demonstrate good intentions and also
to give a financial impetus to colonial development. Local legislative
councils thereafter appeared in many forms, each allowing a forum in
which local discontent could be expressed. Under the banner of com-
promise and conciliation the colonial authorities sought the support of
the new urban elite, professional and commercial, to help make development successful.

They thus sacrificed the rural leadership, the traditional "chiefs"
upon whom they had so strongly depended in the interwar years of
indirect rule at a time when the chief function of empire was mainte-
nance of order, the *pax colonia*. Moreover, there is an element of irony
worth considering here. Much of what was the chiefdom system in
Africa was of European formation, a development of what has been
called the "invention of tradition." Not fully understanding African
leadership designations and equally anxious to provide local authority
with significant trappings of office, the Europeans devised the concept
of "chief," and the holder of the title was invested with an authority
that also included ceremonials that the Europeans thought both appropriate and essential. In viewing African ways through their own eyes,
the Europeans found what was not there; they "invented" a past.[5]

Not "invented" but emerging principally from an urban environment,
most of the new local leaders were "Europeanized," trained in
European-defined professions, fluent in European languages and con-
fident in expressing European ideas. Their significance was such that
they acquired generic nicknames: WOG (White, oriental gentleman) in
Southeast Asia and "Black men in White clothes" in Africa. As jour-
nalists and lawyers, as schoolteachers and medical doctors, they were
often partially integrated into the colonial system and, later, totally
alienated from it. Certainly, one of the most interesting among them
was Vo Nguyen Giap, eventual leader of the Vietminh military victory
over the French in Indochina. Expelled from the prestigious Lycée
National at Hué because of political agitation, he later took a degree in
law at the University of Hanoi. From there he worked both as a history
teacher and a journalist. He met Ho Chi Minh while both were political refugees in China in 1940. Returning to Vietnam in 1944, Giap
organized the first Vietminh military units. His new career took him
from city to countryside.

The city was the concentrated setting for the drama of decolonization, while the countryside provided a more expansive stage. Protest
marches and riots were necessarily urban phenomena characterized by
rather easily amassed numbers and well-established teleological or

focused space, significant points of convergence, as would be a long avenue or a public square. One significant and particularly tragic instance of this urban protest occurred at Setif in Algeria, beginning on May 8, 1945, one day after the war in Europe had ended and local French were in celebration. Then a large crowd of Muslims appeared on the scene to protest against colonial rule. A confused and brutal encounter occurred between the two groups and lasted until French troops restored order five days later. The number of dead was estimated to be between 1,000 and 6,000. Perhaps the most infamous of such urban protests occurred in Sharpeville, South Africa, in 1960 when a non-violent protest against the pass laws (restrictive of African movement in the cities) led to police firing on the crowd, killing 69 and wounding another 178, most struck in the back. A few days later, some 30,000 Africans appeared in Cape Town, near the legislative building, to protest against police brutality.

More significant in the chain of events was the grave incident at Soweto, a township outside Johannesburg, where in 1976 a group of protesting students was fired upon by police. African anger over this occurrence, which included the death of a thirteen-year-old boy, intensified and spread, both strengthening the oppositional ANC (African National Congress) and creating a national situation of unrest that the government was no longer able to manage. Some historians date the beginning of the end of the apartheid regime from this event.

Between these two South African outbursts of protest and severe repression, there were many more. Site of European colonial rule and place of population concentration, the city was the obvious setting for colonial protest. Within its streets were gathered the conditions of dissatisfaction: concentrations of population, most precariously employed at best; communications networks, from newspapers to voluntary associations, such as soccer teams and burial clubs, binding members of a particular ethnic group together; trade unions, notably in British and French possessions (and forbidden in the Belgian Congo and the Portuguese colonies), organizing strikes; the most visible signs of colonial power, such as a parliament building or a governor-general's palace. In sum the conditions for mass protest were urban based.

If the drama was in the city, the more enduring and successful confrontation was in the countryside. Terrorist activities and guerrilla warfare, as practiced in the colonial world, were based in the rural areas. There the large and usually well-equipped forces available to the colonial powers could not be effectively concentrated; and, equally, the smaller numbers of participants and the lesser amount of modern military equipment available to the insurgents made the countryside an easier place in which to find security and build defenses against the colonial power.

Guerrilla warfare beset the colonial Asian territories from the end of World War II. The Dutch in Indonesia from 1946 to 1948, the British in Malaya from 1948 to 1953, and the French in Indochina from 1946 to 1954 encountered stiff resistance to the reinstallation of colonial rule. The British successfully concluded their operations in Malaya against what was essentially a communist-inspired insurgency. However, the Dutch were militarily hard-pressed by indigenous forces and then were threatened by an American decision to deny a needed loan if they did not negotiate withdrawal, which they then did in 1948. The conclusion of the French history in Indochina is well known. No strategy, no change of commanders, no commitment of new troops was sufficient to allow the French to check the Vietminh, the revolutionary group founded by Ho Chi Minh with military activities directed by Vo Nguyen Giap. The defeat of the French outpost at Dien Bien Phu on May 7, 1954, with 10,000 prisoners taken, was astonishing to the French; it was also the final straw, leading them to seek peace and to withdraw, both of which they did in that year.

Such militant activities were also starkly evident in Africa. Even though south of the Sahara the last decade of colonialism witnessed a fairly tranquil transfer of power in most of the colonial territories, there were notable violent upheavals and terrorist activities. The most significant and chronicled uprising was of the Mau Mau, a secret Kikuyu organization that engaged in terrorist activity in Kenya. So dispersed and disruptive were its activities, with attacks on settlers constituting its principal mode of action, that the British had to provide a force of 50,000 men to contain it. The result of Mau Mau was the stark realization by the British that the settlers' days were over and that independence was the only reasonable solution to the costly affair.

More drawn out and brutal was the militant activity inspired by resistance to Portuguese rule in Guinea-Bissau and Angola on the west coast of Africa, and Mozambique on the east. In what then seemed arrogant, and now, in retrospect, seems incredible, the Portuguese government under the dictatorship of Antonio Salazar had encouraged and supported White migration to these territories in the 1950s so that the European population went from about 45,000 in 1945 to 450,000 by the 1960s. Ill-educated and poorly trained, this population settled into small-scale farming and jobs in the service sector, such as house servants. Therefore, the distinction in condition between these new arrivals and the indigenous population was essentially monetary, of income gained. However poor they were in fact, the newly arrived Portuguese earned more money than their African counterparts, a belated example of the persistent wage differential that was a feature of the racist society maintained by the Europeans in the colonial world.

With such a considerable investment of limited national wealth and population in the African colonies, the Portuguese were determined to hold on to these territories. Therefore, the national government was left with little choice but to send in large contingents of troops, the number eventually reaching a half-million. The 1960s was when this struggle was most intense, when the Portuguese were never able to achieve significant victory and the African opposition forces were never able to rout the Portuguese. Eventually the liberation movement was successful, when the Portuguese home government fell under the burden of the war. The new national leadership decided to end colonial rule, largely as the result of international pressure.

The end of French rule in Algeria was not dissimilar in terms of the encounter of rival forces and the effect of that encounter on national politics. In 1958, after four years of struggle against the insurgents, the Fourth Republic in France was swept into historical obscurity. General de Gaulle was recalled to power as a sort of national savior. With his presence and through his determined effort, the Fifth Republic, the current political system of France, was instituted in 1958. In 1962 de Gaulle's government negotiated a peace settlement and a French withdrawal from Algeria.

The events and activities leading up to this outcome are subsumed under "the war without a name," the term so used because the government never declared war and fought the insurgents as if in a police action that therefore allowed the use of conscripts.

The bitter and ferocious encounter began on November 1, 1954, just six months after the French debacle at Dien Bien Phu. It was then that the leadership of the FLN (National Liberation Front) launched an attack, which the French quickly put down and considered to be just another confinable uprising. It was not. Eventually the most severe and enduring of colonial struggles, it was waged first most intensely in the cities and thereafter in the countryside. The urban struggle was effectively won by the French when in 1957 French soldiers, acting on government orders to prevent a planned general strike, moved quickly through the city of Algiers and destroyed the FLN base there. For the next few years the war was fought across the countryside, with French efforts at enforcing order resulting in about 2 million peasants being forced into military camps in a brutal effort at containment. It appeared that the French were about to win the war, with their commitment of about 500,000 soldiers, both professional and conscript, to the effort.

However, widely publicized massacres and atrocities led critics in France to complain that French behavior in Algeria was similar to that of the Nazis during the Occupation. To this growing sense of discontent were added the ill-effects of an abortive effort of the French military in Algeria to stage a revolt in support of the French settlers. Wisely assessing the dismal scene, the Gaullist government realized that a negotiated peace was the only viable solution. In the Evian Accords of 1962 this was achieved.

The militant peasantry and the war-ridden countryside that had created such a stark landscape in Algeria were logical – and dreadful – outcomes of the colonial situation and the reaction to it. As Giap wrote of the situation in Vietnam in his now classic work, *People's War, People's Army* (1961), "a backward country such as ours where peasants make up the majority of the population" is one in which "a people's war is essentially *a peasants' war under the leadership of the working class*" [italics in original]. Minus the Marxist rhetoric about the leadership of the working class, the statement rang true and might therefore be considered a generalization suitable to almost all such agitation in the final decades of colonial empire. The peasantry were concerned about the land problem, their alienation from their place of work and residence when land was converted into private property controlled by the colonialists. Land reform, made a major part of the Vietminh political program, was a key issue in all efforts at liberation from colonialism.

As an explanation of the land issue in Algeria, Frantz Fanon wrote *The Wretched of the Earth*. In his critical view of the colonial situation, the socio-economic order was bifurcated: there existed a small group of intellectuals, urban based, who, while professing concern with national liberation, were essentially self-serving: "they organize the loot of whatever national resources exist." Only when the intellectual leaves the city to arouse support in the countryside is "he struck with wonder and amazement" at the honesty and truth that he finds among the people there. That truth was bread and land, the realization of the basic needs and purposes that characterized those who worked the soil.

Perhaps unintentionally, Fanon helped reawaken the populist myth earlier found in American and European thought by transposing it to the contemporary colonial world, Algeria in particular. The goodness emanating from the land and the alienation generated in the city were the stark contrasts of the modern world, described in the literature of the Third World in the late twentieth century as they had been in the literature of the First World in the late nineteenth century. The colonial city, described by Fanon's fellow countryman, Aimé Césaire, in his epic poem *Return to My Native Land* (1938) as "winded under the geometric weight of its eternally renewed cross," was seen as an alien, incomprehensible place. "This city is no place for me. I am lost in it." These are the words of the husband of the principal character in Kamal Markandaya's widely acclaimed work, *Nectar in a Sieve*. First published in 1954, this novel is part of a literary genre of social realism that was the main form of the first generation of post-colonial fiction. The dichotomy between countryside and city that had figured into the works of Charles Dickens and Honoré de Balzac, that was politically significant in the American populist movement of the late nineteenth century, became an important part of the cultural legacy of the colonial experience.

When Fanon speaks in *The Wretched of the Earth* of the "know-all, smart, wily intellectuals," he is describing a type of individual that was widely perceived as existing in this dichotomous landscape and an individual who was, in American slang, once called "the city slicker," that person out to serve himself, to reap the benefits of often illicit transactions in an environment dominated by the cash nexus. In the saga-novels of Chinua Achebe, which follow the fate of the Okonkwo family, the corrupting influence of the city is described; and the simpler, communally binding experience of the countryside is considered, if not praised, as a more comforting alternative.

The Eurafrican and Eurasian cities were commercial, driven by a capitalist market economy. As one of the characters in *The Swamp Dwellers*, a one-act play by the Nigerian author Wole Soyinka, says of the young who leave the villages: "It ruins them. The city ruins them. What did they seek there except money?"

The question was asked by new national leaders in Africa just as colonial empire retreated. Their response was an ideology of African socialism, the contention that the precolonial African environment had fostered a cooperative rather than a competitive approach to economic development. Theirs was a socialism of community, not of class struggle. Fervently expressed, African socialism was seen as a new "link" ideology, one that could bring together the disparate ethnic and economic units within the former colonial territory to form in spirit a new nation. Tom Mboya, minister of labor in Kenya in the year of its independence (1963), wrote: "We need a new political philosophy – a philosophy of our own – that will explain, validify, and help to cement our experience."

Little has come of the ideology, its proponents now gone, its intentions swept away by contemporary global culture characterized by the production of consumer goods, the growth of the tourist industry, and the emergence of the international conglomerate. In certain cities, Hong

Kong and Singapore most obviously, the new era has meant previously untold prosperity, the numerous and closely aligned skyscrapers standing as the high marks of this change. Older and sleepier places, like Nassau in the Bahamas or Papeete in Tahiti, have acquired some economic vitality and redirected purpose as ports-of-call for the most recently successful cruise ship industry. As the colonial enterprise folded up and fell down in Asia, European hope was briefly transferred to Sub-Saharan Africa where investment in real estate and the promise it still seemed to offer in the 1950s led to the verticalization of the hitherto ground-hugging cityscape. The tall buildings of the so-called "international style," starkly functional and enrobed in glass walls, gave to the major colonial cities a strikingly similar appearance of modernity. In this sense Singapore and Hong Kong may be considered the most astounding achievements of an urban environment that went from tile roofs and iron-railed balconies to steel frames soaring dozens of stories above the old places of maritime commerce to the new spaces of global finance.

Such efforts continued in big vertical spurts immediately after independence, as notable in Africa as in Asia. Novelist V. S. Naipaul, a severe critic of postcolonial development, allowed one of the characters in *A Bend in the River* (1979) to complain: "We can trample on the past . . . That is what most of the leaders of Africa do. They want to build skyscrapers in the bush."

More broadly the condition of the postcolonial city is, however, the intensification of earlier problems, those that preceded the era of high rises. The continuing influx of population from countryside to city has been outpaced by the rise of birth rates in the urban areas so as to create a housing shortage and slums of incredible proportions. In 1959 about one-eighth of the population of Delhi, some 200,000 individuals, was living in *bustees*, hastily constructed shacks. The problem was comparable elsewhere. It joined a number of other problems to make postcolonial urbanization one of the major global concerns: traffic congestion and air pollution intensified as postcolonial cities motorized; sewer systems and water supplies, never adequate, were overstressed by unplanned usage; the broad infrastructure of the city, notably its streets, tended to decay because of neglect, in turn the result of insufficient funds for such public services.

In retrospect, the historian may state that the ambivalent relationship of countryside to city in the colonial period did not alter greatly in the time of decolonization. The challenge of realignment, of better balance, is one that had been much discussed and has not yet been successfully addressed.

6 "Gotta be this or that"

The problems of independence

There was one particular resplendent moment in the early years of decolonization. It occurred on March 6, 1957, when Ghana obtained its independence. At one minute after midnight the Union Jack was lowered and the red, green, and gold flag of Ghana raised. Later, at the official ceremonies during the bright light of day, the Duchess of Kent, representing Queen Elizabeth, declared: "My government in the United Kingdom have ceased from today to have any authority in Ghana." Kwame Nkrumah, new prime minister, responded: "We part from the former imperial power." Two thousand official representatives from all over the world attended the lavish independence day celebrations. In the evening, on the marbled floor of the new State House, the Duchess and the Prime Minister briefly danced together to the song, "Gotta Be This or That."

The general assumption of all there gathered was that it "gotta be this": independence, improvement, beneficial rule for all. Here was to be a "revolution of expectations," a popular phrase of the period describing the high hopes for a new postcolonial order. Nkrumah gave rhetorical emphasis to this change through his use of the traditional nautical metaphor by which he concluded his autobiography, published in the year of independence:

> And I, as I proudly stand on the bridge of that lone vessel as she confidently sets sail, I raise a hand to shade my eyes from the glaring African sun and scan the horizon. There is so much more beyond.

Within nine years the Nkrumah government was shipwrecked, overthrown as inefficient, corrupt, and authoritarian. The experience of Ghana was neither unique nor unusual. Throughout Africa and much of Asia in the next two decades, the final ones of decolonization, the cultural landscape was bleak. Disorder and oppression, the military *coup d'état* and dictatorship were frequent, almost commonplace.

Human rights were violated and massive repressive measures were not unusual. Poverty and urban unemployment increased. Most economies performed poorly and infrastructure crumbled, with unrepaired roads seemingly an endemic condition.

The notable exceptions to this state of affairs were India, where democracy performed well, even if the economy did not; and the "four little dragons" (also called the "gang of four") of Singapore, Hong Kong, Taiwan, and Korea, where the economies functioned superbly even though the political systems were not particularly commendable, Hong Kong perhaps excepted.

Elsewhere, "instability" became the generic term to describe this set of unfavorable conditions so widespread throughout the former colonial world. The new states seemed to have both inherited the wind and been bequeathed the imperial debris. They were ill prepared for the onrush of problems from without and constrained by the colonial structures and institutions found within. Unlike the first decolonized country of the late eighteenth century, the United States, those decolonized countries of the late twentieth century were not and could not pretend to be part of a "new world."

Nkrumah's metaphor of the ship of state was significant because it was anachronistic: there was no horizon toward which to sail; there was no lonely sea to cross. The world was, quite simply, filled up. The postcolonial responsibility was essentially to undo the clutter: crowded cities, unemployment, trade imbalance, inefficient bureaucracies, insufficient educational establishments. And yet all such needful activities were largely constrained or twisted by a global economic system itself undergoing major change.

The growth period of the international economy took place in the two decades in which decolonization occurred and ended abruptly with the oil crisis of 1973 when the international cartel OPEC (Organization of Petroleum Exporting Countries) both raised prices and curtailed production, thus creating an energy shortage which most adversely affected the new postcolonial countries that had based the forward movement of their own economic engines on that fuel. The condition was further aggravated by the fall in prices for other raw materials and for agricultural products, the mainstay of so many of the economies of these countries, economies that were in effect still colonial in nature. Perhaps more significant was the emergence of a global agricultural economy. Developed nations, the United States in particular, were exporting grain in large quantities to the former colonial regions, which demanded wheat, for instance, because of changes in diet and nutrition. Such a generalization was not true, however, for Sub-Saharan Africa where chronic food shortage was a major concern. The montage of causes there produced a gloomy picture. With soils often too poor to allow any appreciable increase in agricultural output, with population growth resulting from improved medical conditions and better hygiene, with population shifts to urban areas reducing the rural labor supply, with such urban development requiring more food, and with governmental policy directed to export cash crops (bananas and cocoa, among the most obvious), Sub-Saharan Africa was grey with despair.

Given the range of economic disparity existing among nations in the postcolonial era, Western analysts considered the need to redivide the world into horizontal components of economic success – or lack thereof. Designations of "rich" and "poor" nations or "industrial" and "non-industrial" no longer sufficed. There were now four categories: "developed nations," "newly developing nations," "less developed nations," and "least developed nations" – this last category implying a state of economic hopelessness.

Such divisions were only delineated in the last twenty years when global experts began to realize that international relations were no longer dominantly political but were heavily influenced by economic issues. The old eighteenth-century term "political economy" was reinvented to describe the new importance of international trade and commercial arrangements, the new role of the state in fostering research and the creation of new industries, the new significance of multinational corporations as "actors" on the world stage.

This brief assessment of a very complicated and unstable world condition is meant to stand as a preface to the developments required of and desired by the former colonial territories, now standing as independent states.

What is now obvious, if it was not then seen in the afterglow of the setting imperial sun, is that most of the first generation of political leaders were not up to the new global tasks thrust upon them. These people and their governmental cohorts were not formally trained nor disposed by experience to be managers or technocrats. They were trained in what are called the "liberal professions" – law, education, and journalism – with some schooled in medicine as well. Their supporters also ranged along a narrow occupational spectrum, not for the most part professional. This group included the petty bourgeoisie (the famous "market women" of Ghana, for instance) and guerrilla fighters. Few if any in high government office were schooled or experienced in the field of international finance or commerce. There were no local equivalents of the Eurocrats, that new breed of technocrats who viewed industry beyond national boundaries, and of whom Jean Monnet, instrumental in forming the European Coal and Steel Community in 1951, is always selected as exemplary.

The power elite in the newly emerging states was, for its time, unusually one-dimensional, skilled in most aspects of political behavior and tactics. Moreover, it treated national and international affairs as continuing matters of diplomacy and ideology, considered essentially as postcolonial and not post-modern. Moreover, the so-called political base upon which the new political power rested was limited in scope and unstable at best. The well-known and much described Western bourgeoisie which both motivated and controlled the economies of the "developed" nations was nearly non-existent in most of the former colonies. Its closest analogue was an administrative middle class, its revenue not generated but derived, its members salaried bureaucrats. Well-developed and organized labor forces were another exception; and the new state apparatus often sought to eliminate or subsume under state control such organizations, as indeed quickly happened in Ghana where the labor movement was both broken and alienated when a strike in 1961 was forcibly ended by the government. In Tanganyika the ruling party TANU (Tanganyika African National Union) abolished the labor union and set in place its own state-controlled apparatus.

Moreover, the lack of radical or revolutionary change in colonially predetermined institutions and structures was a major consideration. With the possible exception of Ho Chi Minh's Vietnam the state structure and the administrative form remained essentially what they had been. The national state, cynics would remark, was only the colony fitted out with a new flag. (The frequently employed expression was "flag sovereignty.") The obvious changes were lateral moves, as Asians and Africans went from the outside to the inside, as the offices once held by Europeans as colonial administrators became those held by Asians and Africans as state ministers. Frantz Fanon denounced this condition in *The Wretched of the Earth*: "The native bourgeoisie that comes to power uses its class aggressiveness to corner the positions formerly kept by foreigners." Fanon's fear was that the new nationalism might be as self-serving as had been the old colonialism.

Politically alert, economically uncertain, the new leadership doubly depended on Europeans and Americans: first, for financial assistance in realizing development plans; and, second, for the technological advice to realize them. What truly confounded the issue was obvious: economic growth was preceding economic development. To generate new financial resources for the state, the increase of "colonial" produce was encouraged, not diversification of the economy or, more pressingly, the guarantee of sufficient crops to meet the needs of national consumption. (In Nigeria, for instance, in the first decade after independence, agricultural production decreased by 2 per cent from its level in the last year of colonial rule. The situation of Ghana was little better: an increase of 0.3 per cent in the first postcolonial decade was dismally followed by a 3.1 per cent decrease in the second decade.) The single-crop economy of colonial days thus continued. The bananas of the Ivory Coast, the tea of Sri Lanka (formerly Ceylon), the peanuts of Senegal increased in number of tons yielded but prices did not increase commensurately. One of the most commented on examples was of cocoa in Ghana where the tonnage increased from 350,000 in 1960 to 495,000 in 1965 with little appreciable increase in farmers' incomes. This seeming disparity of more produced and little more gained resulted from a decline in world market prices for most raw materials in the 1960s and 1970s and because of the continuing foreign control of these raw materials by profit-seeking corporations based in Europe or America.

Growth also inhibited where it did not preclude development. The lack of what has been called "technology transfer" was significant. In Ghana at the time of independence when cocoa was the major export product, there was only one Ghanaian horticulturalist. In the Belgian Congo at the time of independence, there were not even ten Africans with university degrees and fewer than 200,000 individuals who had finished high school. Technological positions were retained or assumed by Europeans and, now, by Americans as well. Urban planners, economists, and engineers carried their thoughts and their baggage to the Third World countries, while American universities established centers of research abroad to assist with the multifaceted process called "modernization."

Few of the new national leaders were prepared for or predisposed to careful consideration of the problems that independence brought. Almost all of these individuals, the "founding fathers" of their nations, fared poorly at their new-found tasks. Their experience had been principally colonial and acquired in three phases. First, these later leaders stood as young reformers or opponents of the colonial system, primarily from the position of being students within it and writers of tracts, articles, and books about or against it. Second, they assumed positions of leadership of movements or parties seeking reform or demanding independence. Those in the latter category were often deemed subversive by the colonial authorities and were therefore frequently imprisoned. This group, consisting of individuals as geographically diverse as Nehru of India, Ben Bella of Algeria, and Nkrumah of the Gold Coast (Ghana), formed a cohort described as "prison graduates." Of this number, the most unusual in sentence received and spirit maintained is Nelson Mandela, who became president of the Republic of South Africa. Mandela was imprisoned from 1962 to 1991 and yet emerged from this horrendous experience to become the most respected, effective, and conciliatory of the modern African leaders. Third, members of this political cohort were tolerated, allowed, or even encouraged as they sought national independence, working within the colonial system in order to eliminate it. There is widespread agreement, for instance, that the reason why the transition of power in Ghana went so smoothly was the cooperation and friendship established between the last British governor of the colony, Charles Arden-Clarke, and Kwame Nkrumah.

In one lifetime the cycle of political devolution occurred. Or, better, between youth and middle age, the new national leaders had participated in major historic change. As men in their forties and fifties, they assumed the authority they had long struggled to have, as in the case of Ho Chi Minh; or they were moved by the currents of the time from cooperative outsider to independent leader. One instance of this latter coincidence of biography and nationhood may serve to make the point. President Leopold Sedar Senghor of Senegal, born in 1906, was a university student in Paris in the 1920s. He there encountered African-Americans like the poet Langston Hughes who were celebrating the Harlem Renaissance, the literary movement that, it might be said, gave lyrical voice to the phrase coined by Marcus Garvey, "Black is beautiful." In the late 1930s Senghor became a literature teacher at the prestigious Lycée Louis le Grand in Paris; he then served as a solider in the French army (and was taken as a prisoner of war) in 1939–40. Elected after the war as a representative from Senegal to the French National Assembly, he served as one of the grammarians for the Constitution of the Fourth Republic and soon acquired the title and office of minister in the government of Premier Edgar Faure, 1955–6. Senghor was then president of Senegal from 1960 to 1980. His productive lifetime spanned the era of decolonization, the fifty years between the 1920s and the 1970s.

Whatever their experience and intentions, each of the leaders in Senghor's political class was confronted with the difficulty of structuring new political institutions, of finding means to create a sense of national unity, and of assuring the economic betterment of the country. The task was formidable, the results too often short of the many desires and demands voiced by diverse segments of the population. Illiteracy and venality compounded the national situation. Obi Okonkwo, the hero of Chinua Achebe's novel *No Longer at Ease*, is a bright, well-trained idealist who sees in Nigeria a country lost in ignorance and corruption, hence unlikely to achieve democracy. And yet he concludes with some hope, "England was once like this."

The truth of his statement cannot be questioned. However, it was the striking and widely publicized contrast between the rhetoric of independence and the occurrence of corruption that made the matter so politically debilitating in the postcolonial situation. Nkrumah was not the only leader to fall over such an issue. Unlike Senghor, who voluntarily left the office of president, many of the others were overthrown or ousted, their policies and practices found to be inadequate, corrupt, or anti-democratic. In round numbers and raw figures, some 75 *coups d'état*, mostly military in nature, occurred in the former colonial world in the first three decades of independence. Ghana underwent three between 1966 and 1972; Nigeria, two in 1966 alone. Military leaders appeared in Indonesia and the Philippines, in Algeria and Zaire, these here mentioned to suggest the geographical range of the phenomenon.

Earlier analyzed as a sign of grave political instability and a gross failure of democratic institutions – most obviously, the "Westminster system," or the form of parliamentary government which the British proudly listed as their gift to the new nations – more recent research suggests that military rule resulted because the army, as one of the few well-organized, well-trained, and nationwide groups, could serve as "guardian," "broker," or "gatekeeper," could attempt to bring back on course errant civilian governments that had failed in creating a sense of unity, that had failed to achieve economic betterment.[1]

However, the record of military leadership became one of military dictatorship, a condition that was prominent for two decades. The 1970s and 1980s were the years of rule by those called the "Big Men": authoritarian, ruthless, self-serving. Among this substantial group three stand out vividly. The first was Idi Amin who terrorized the population of Uganda as its ruler from 1971 to 1979, and who brutally forced out the Indian population of the country and exterminated his political opposition. The second was Emperor Bokassa I (formerly a military officer named Jean Bedel Bokasso) who had been president of the Central African Republic since 1965 but who, rather in imitation of Napoleon, took the title of emperor in 1976 and indulged in an elaborate coronation ceremony in 1977 that has been estimated to have cost one-quarter of the nation's annual income. He was finally overthrown on September 21, 1979, after his regime killed some 100 schoolchildren who were protesting about the price of school uniforms that Bokassa had both designed and demanded must be worn. The third figure, the longest in power and most devastating in effect, was Mobutu Sese Seketo, who as president of the country he named Zaire from 1965 until 1997 oppressed his people, imprisoned his opposition, and drained the nation of its wealth, with his personal financial worth estimated in billions of dollars. Zaire, now the Democratic Republic of the Congo, was the richest African nation in terms of natural resources. At the end of Mobutu's reign, its population was one of the poorest.

However, it was the economic condition, more than any other factor, that has aggravated the political situation and has denied the hopes of those who saw decolonization as the opening of a new era. With the notable exceptions of the "four little dragons," those economically successful small states that have become major industrial and financial powers with a high standard of living, grouped along the Pacific Rim where geographical location has been a major advantage, the new nations did not significantly improve themselves over their previous colonial situation in the first two decades of independence. In the decade of the 1990s, however, Malaysia and India have moved dramatically forward in the field of computer technology, while part of Sub-Saharan Africa has also enjoyed improvement with increased private investment and new economic leadership.

In explanation of the lack of better economic performance after independence, the theory of "neo-colonialism" was widely posited. One of the most popular, if not original, explanations of this condition was Kwame Nkrumah's book *Neo-colonialism, The Last Stage of Imperialism* (1965). Just as Lenin "updated" Marx to explain the persistence of capitalism, so Nkrumah "updated" Lenin to explain the persistence of imperialism in a new guise. As he states: "The result of neo-colonialism is that foreign capital is used for the exploitation rather than for the development of the less developed parts of the world." Less blatant, more subtle, and therefore all the more pernicious than its predecessor colonialism, neo-colonialism, goes the argument, locks the former colonial territories into positions of client states of the major industrial-capitalist powers. Nkrumah singles out the United States as "the very citadel of neo-colonialism." The control that it maintains is assured through capital loans, domination of the world market and international aid. Nkrumah protests this condition, as his book indicates; and his turn to the political left in the last years of his administration is in part a result of his perceptions.

On a broader scale, imperialism and colonialism have been seen as functions of a "world capitalist system" that has developed and expanded until it reaches around the world and into every nation. In such an analysis the older core–periphery argument first used by the imperialists themselves to explain global expansion is now redesigned as the template of a global economic theory. In a bitter analysis of this condition cast in terms of development and underdevelopment, the Guyanese scholar Walter Rodney explained, as the title of his book states, *How Europe Underdeveloped Africa* (1972). "Imperialism" was for him nothing other than "the extended capitalist system, which for many years embraced the whole world." It was through this economic exploitation that the Western nations, mindful of their own position of economic advantage and needful of the raw materials of Africa, "underdeveloped" that continent, set it back economically by prohibiting its healthy and beneficial growth.

In all too many nation states newly emerged from their colonial status, sovereignty in principle has not allowed independence of action in fact. The geography of the situation and the current condition of the global economy seem to have prohibited this attainment, even if the condition does not result from direct conspiracy, as some of the critics would have it.

In current global economic analysis, arguments such as those proposed by Nkrumah and Rodney have only historical significance; they are otherwise irrelevant. The contemporary situation is one now described as "post neo-colonialism." Not the former colonial conditions but the current global ones configure and control the world. Most obviously, the NICs ("newly industrializing countries"), of which Singapore and Korea seem the most striking, have assumed a place in the world market vaster than their physical size would seem to allow. With high gross income products and an ever-increasing individual standard of living, these small states fall into the category that was once labeled "Western." Conversely, many areas of the world exploited by the "West" in its imperialist era are now without much interest to European or American capitalists. Much of Sub-Saharan Africa has been "marginalized," deprived both of the assistance and investment that had rushed in during the 1970s. Visiting South Africa in March 1997, the wife of the president of the United States, Hillary Clinton, acknowledged this problem when she stated that "we have to rethink that engagement [formed by the Cold War and oppressive African regimes] and determine what the United States can do to help countries like South Africa and others . . . to move toward democracy and self-sufficiency."

Whatever that thinking may be, and wherever considered, it will not follow the line of progress that was so praised as the previous century closed. Today's global pattern is seen, if seen at all, rather like a vast game of cat's cradle: the linear combinations of social and economic development, of transnational activities, are being reworked to form new and inconstant designs. The position of the United States as the world's chief debtor nation is some proof of this change, and so is the remarkable increase in the export trade from China in the last ten years. The remarkable success of the Korean automobile and electronics industries would be still another, as would be the shift in trade balance between the United States and Mexico, which now favors Mexico.

From this newly reworked pattern of global political and economic power and position, no simple conclusion is possible. Only this much is certain: imperialism and colonialism as ideologies justifying policies and institutions designed to ensure economic advantage through imposed political control are henceforth historical phenomena. In this sense, decolonization is complete.

Standing as proof of a new era and proclaimed as a sign of the advent of the shift of world power to Asia are the Petronas Towers in Kuala Lampur, Malaysia. Completed in 1997, these twin towers stand at 1,483 feet each. They are the tallest buildings in the world and expressive of new corporate wealth, a measure of Malaysia's recent industrial success, particularly as the principal exporter of computer semiconductors. The buildings, part of a new urban complex under construction, are situated on the grounds of the old Selangor Turf Club which, as part of the British colonial legacy, raced thoroughbred horses until 1992, when the sound of hooves was replaced by that of bulldozers; when the not-so-old in this part of the world noisily gave way to the very new.

7 Outside in
Colonial migration

Major demographic shifts accompanied the end of colonial empire. As the Europeans left, so did many of their former colonial subjects. The statistics defining such movements are staggering: over 16 million individuals within the former colonial world changed their place of residence in scarcely more than three decades and did so as often out of despair as with hope. The result was the severe complication of urban patterns, the aggravation of racism, the enrichment of culture. Shanty towns and ghettos sprawled, race riots erupted in London and Paris, Indian restaurants in London and Indonesian ones in Amsterdam changed the dining-out habits of the populations of these cities. A forced cosmopolitanism grew in Europe – and in Australia, as well as the United States and Canada – as political refugees and persons seeking economic opportunities came by the boatful. If there was a moment that marked this still unsettling and resettling trend, it was in May 1948 when the ship *Empire Windrush* brought 417 Jamaicans to London, the first such number at one time. By 1980 some 1.5 million people from the former empire, exclusive of the White immigrants from places like Ireland and Canada, had settled in the island kingdom. By then an equal number of Algerians and Africans had uncertainly settled in France.

People moved either because they wanted to or because they had to. Theorists suggest that the determinant of the former group was rather like a personalized form of double-entry bookkeeping in which the deficit features of remaining home were outweighed by the potential assets of moving away. In addition, there was the effect of a small range of factors amounting to compulsion: pressure for a young person to make money in order to support the family, population growth and resulting unemployment in the home region, fear of political oppression from an unfriendly regime. The "push–pull" theory of migration is the most useful of generalizations: unfavorable conditions at home urged people to move away, anticipated attractions of another country directed them outward. Certainly, the rage of modernization – urban growth, development policies, industrialization, advanced communications and health services – was a powerful factor leading to easy placement of foreign arrivals in those service sectors of the economy vacated by nationals seeking and finding advancement in other occupations. Street cleaners and cooks, delivery men and taxi drivers, and everywhere street vendors, such were the most common forms of employment. Many of the arrivals had limited-duration work permits; they were meant to be temporary workers, not permanent residents. In Germany they were called *gastarbeiter*, "guest workers," most of whom were Italian and Turkish but with more than a sprinkling among them of arrivals from the colonial areas.

These people formed what might be called the second (and large) generation of immigrants from the colonial and former colonial territories. They followed a smaller number, the first generation, that was far more privileged in condition and definitely temporary in status. These were for the most part the students who appeared in the interwar period – Senghor and Nehru, for instance – who sought educational opportunity and cultural advantage; their chief intention was to gain advancement within the colonial situation and then, for many, to return home to encourage their own and their people's causes.

Their idealism was tempered by their ambitions. In the last decade of imperialism, they appeared in considerable numbers, with a university degree or, more simply, attendance at a European university, seen as a sort of passepartout, the means to multiple opportunities at home. Many are the stories of the "beentos," the English-schooled young men, those who had "been to" London in the last decades of colonial empire, who returned home to West Africa with an affected style that included dressing in English worsteds and starched collars, regardless of the temperature and humidity. When Obi Okonkwo, in Achebe's *No Longer at Ease*, appears at a reception of the Umuofia Progressive Union, the organization that had raised the money to send him to England and now was proudly waiting to greet him, he was dressed in shirtsleeves, certainly appropriate to the weather but most certainly not to the occasion. As he saw the neatly dressed group awaiting him, Obi realized he had made a mistake: "Everybody expected a young man from England to be impressively turned out."

Before their successors arrived in great numbers and with different purposes, the earlier visitors from the colonies to the metropolitan country were usually treated indifferently or considerately. One of the characters in Forster's *A Passage to India* remarks on the kindness shown him by a couple when he was in England: "They were father and mother to me . . . On the vacations their Rectory became my home." With mass immigration to Europe, the enthusiasm or condescension shown to the few gave way to the disdain and contempt for the many. As a result racism became more widespread in open expression and more complicated in effect. What aggravated the matter were two new conditions: the influx of political refugees and the arrival of the families of immigrant workers.

A late twentieth-century diaspora of people violently uprooted occurred, as political power was reallocated and old ethnic antagonisms resurfaced. The thin veneer of the *pax colonia* quickly cracked. In its first and most horrendous manifestation, the conclusion of the British Raj, India was violently cleft in two. The administrative decision to allow a division largely on the basis of Hindu and Muslim religious preferences led to the creation of two new states, India and Pakistan. As a result of this political change, some 7.5 million people, it is estimated, moved from one area to the other and some 1 million were killed in accompanying riots and assassinations. The intensity of this movement is statistically revealed in an unintended use of the well-known device of imperial control: some 2.3 million individuals were moved by train from one new country to the other in fewer than three months, between August 27 and November 6, 1947.

Elsewhere, there were similarly forced movements, if none quite so numerically distended as that in India. When in 1948 British rule ended in Palestine and the state of Israel came into being, some 419,000 Palestinians left their land. During the brutal dictatorship of Idi Amin in Uganda, 1971–9, some 27,000 Indians, many families resident in that region since the Uganda railroad was built by their labor in the first years of the century, fled to England after being deprived of their property and threatened with loss of life. Across the globe, in former French Indochina, an estimated 400,000 Vietnamese fled their land in the years 1975–9, as the Vietminh took over after the departure of the Americans. This particular emigration (largely achieved on small boats, hence the description of the refugees as "boat people") followed upon the migration, north and south, of some 1 million Vietnamese after the Geneva Accords of 1954 that divided the country in two in the aftermath of the French defeat at Dien Bien Phu.

No demographic shift was more unusual than that which occurred among the colonials themselves, the European settlers principally from the Netherlands and France who had long resided abroad and now found themselves in the category of the "repatriated," but brought back by circumstance, not desire, to an environment largely alien to them in all but language spoken and citizenship held. Theirs is a history still inadequately told but now ended, as both groups have been assimilated into the "homeland" culture.

The repatriated Dutch had a slightly longer and more complicated history than their French counterparts. It centered on Indonesia, and it began at the end of the Japanese conquest when some residents on the islands sought temporary refuge in the Netherlands in face of the political turmoil of nationalist resistance to the re-establishment of Dutch rule. With independence achieved in 1949, a larger influx occurred, with about 180,000 "Indos," as the Indo-Dutch were called, settling in the Netherlands.

The situation of the Algerian *repatriés* was more dramatic, because greater in scale and more rapid in occurrence. About 1 million French citizens hastily left Algeria as the French government turned over authority to the new Algerian republic in 1962. A group of mixed ancestry that included Spanish, Italians, and Maltese, these persons, known as *pieds noirs* after the cheap black shoes they often wore, went to a France they scarcely knew and settled as best they could in an environment that they found alien. Most came through the port of Marseilles where approximately 100,000 settled, while the rest were scattered throughout the country, with the largest settlement in the south of France, a region environmentally comparable to the North African world that they had known.

Both the repatriated Dutch and the French were accompanied by a much smaller but less successfully integrated group of indigenous population that had supported the colonial effort. In the Netherlands these were called the Amonese, from the south islands of Indonesia; they had mostly served in the Royal Dutch Indonesian Army. With independence, they were either integrated into the new national army or given the choice of being demobilized. In a remarkable law suit, those who did not wish to remain in Indonesia under either of these two options sought asylum in the Netherlands. The Dutch court upheld their suit, and some 13,000 entered the Netherlands where they settled in separate encampments. The French *repatriés* were joined in their resettlement in France by the *harki* (a name derived from an Arabic term for those on the move). These Muslim Algerians were those who had, for reasons of personal advantage as well as political conviction, sided with the French. They numbered about 85,000 and added to the number of North Africans settling in France as permanent residents and as workers.

There were also smaller numbers of immigrants scattered about: about 70,000 Surinamese in the Netherlands; 35,000 Vietnamese and

138,000 from Sub-Saharan Africa in France; and 60,000 Chinese from Hong Kong to Great Britain between 1956 and 1965 – this last number increasing as independence of that crown colony in 1997 drew near. Largest of such groups, and one primarily propelled outward by the search for employment denied them at home, was the multitude of 1.5 million Filipinos who sought work abroad between 1975 and 1985 and who can now be found from Athens to Washington.

The egress of people from the former colonial areas has also had a major impact on the demography of the United States. The 1990 Census Report provided the following figures of such colonial émigrés, a number which demonstrates the increasingly cosmopolitan nature of the American population, already diversified by heavy immigration from Mexico, Cuba and Haiti:

Ethnicity	Number
Filipinos	1,406,770
Asian Indians	815,447
Vietnamese	614,547
Samoans	62,964
Guamians	49,345

Were one to deal in singularities as well in an effort to reach a total count of the displaced persons of the postcolonial era, then deposed rulers could be added to this list. Among the most obvious are: King Farouk of Egypt, who spent his last days on the French Riviera, as did the Emperor Bao Dai, both squandering money on horse races; Kwame Nkrumah of Ghana, who lived the last years of his life in neighboring Guinea where he at least enjoyed the special title of "co-president"; Idi Amin, initially installed in a villa in Tunisia and, more recently, without address in the Sudan; Ferdinand Marcos of the Philippines who arrived ill and soon died on the Hawaiian Islands. The last of this number was Mobutu Sese Seko who was buried in Morocco where he lived briefly before his death.

The domestic and social situation that these individuals enjoyed as exiles was starkly at variance with that endured by most of the newly arrived immigrants in Europe. This group in large measure served as poorly paid workers found at the bottom of the socio-economic structure. To understand the complexity of the situation, one must view it as two-layered or two-phased. The first occurred as colonial empire ended. It ran on in time for what the French have called the "glorious thirty," the three postwar decades in which the much vaunted "economic miracle" or what has also been rather pretentiously labeled the "Second

European Renaissance" occurred. In this final phase of big machine, labor-intensive industrialization, when Volkswagen produced more Beetles than the Ford Motor Company had produced Model-Ts, when the French Caravelle jet aircraft served midwestern American cities, when urban reconstruction led to vast fields of high-rise, state-supported housing, cheap labor was essential. The low-level service occupations vacated by Europeans entering the working middle class were soon filled by immigrants from the colonial areas. Most of them arrived in great numbers but they also arrived alone: they were men who had left their families behind and who required by way of personal comfort, given European definition, little more than a bed in a rundown boarding house.

By the 1980s, however, the second phase of this ingress had occurred. There was then to be seen a new, densely patterned European cityscape. Employment opportunities had declined as postmodern economics, characterized by high-tech industries and multinational corporations, reduced earlier European industrial advantages (the failure to create a competitive European computer industry being the most obvious cause). As migrants from the former colonies now became permanent residents in Europe, they brought their families, so that large numbers, constrained by low wages, lived in overcrowded and run-down neighborhoods in a condition described by the French as *ghettos à l'américain*. Ethnically distinctive enclaves, quite unlike any social arrangement that had existed before in modern Western Europe, now appeared in major cities like Lyon and Liverpool, as well as Paris and London, and furthered a sense of cultural divisiveness. Whole neighborhoods acquired something of the appearance and atmosphere of the culture of Jamaica and Algeria from which the immigrants and their families had come. Family settlement changed the social disposition of the immigrant populations and deeply colored European perceptions of it. V. S. Naipaul, with his clear eye and pessimistic disposition, briefly described the new scene in his novel *The Mimic Men*. As the narrator looks out of a train window he sees "Victorian working-class tenements whose gardens, long abandoned, had for stretches turned into Caribbean backyards."

This permanent residence and, with it, the importation of cultural behavior unfamiliar to those resident in the host country created suspicion and resentment. It was this unplanned and perplexing colonization of the former colonial nations by the former colonial peoples that caused dismay and, worse, race riots, precipitated by angry young Whites as well as by resentful immigrants of color. The riots that erupted in Great Britain in 1981 and again in 1985 were the worst inner-city conflicts that the nation had endured, with Brixton in London and Toxteth in Liverpool principal scenes on both occasions.

These violent expressions of social discontent were joined by new and widespread anti-social attitudes. The increase of crime among unemployed youth was most glaring among the African-Caribbean population, a condition that led to sweeping racist generalization from conservatives and to accusations of police brutality fostered by racist prejudice from the liberals. Such issues were aggravated by the behavior of some unemployed and disenchanted sectors of White youth, notably "skinheads," so called because of their closely shaved scalps, who engaged in personal brutal acts against the immigrants. "Pakki bashing" was the street term for such action in London.

This spontaneous and violent action of opposition was rudely complemented by the appearance of new right-wing political organizations expressing a xenophobia heavily tinctured with racism. Most significant in Britain and France were two unrelated groups sharing a common name: the National Front. In Britain the party had few adherents and little effect, but the French version was more enduring and troublesome. Both national groups were concerned with perceived national decline and what they saw as the ill effects of decolonization (the head of the French National Front, Jean-Marie Le Pen had served as a paratrooper in the French army in Algeria). They assumed decidedly racist attitudes, combining anti-Semitism with opposition to immigration. Both parties equated increasing urban crime, notably mugging and robbery, with the appearance of a first generation of Britons and French who were born of the "tropical immigrants"; both parties saw immigrants as a drain on social welfare programs; both therefore urged strong immigration laws. The National Front was a nettlesome problem in the 1960s and 1970s in Great Britain; the National Front continues to be a source of political concern in contemporary France.

The chief ideologues of racist sentiment in the two countries are Enoch Powell in Britain, a Conservative and subsequently Ulster Unionist Member of Parliament; and Le Pen in France. Powell attained instant notoriety when he gave what is now called his "rivers of blood" speech at Birmingham in 1962, in which he likened future British racial problems to American ones and anticipated the "horror" of such a future resulting from "our own volition and our own neglect." Following the riots of the 1980s, he called for the repatriation of the colored population of the country. Le Pen has blamed most of his nation's ills on the North Africans and Indochinese that have settled in France. Moreover, like Powell in Britain, Le Pen complains that these new immigrants, unlike previous ones, form "separate entities," intentionally distinct from the French. "We are today in the process of losing, through blindness and cowardice of our leaders, our identity as a nation," he was quoted as saying in the *New York Times* (October 4, 1987).

Closely allied with, but not necessarily integrated with such racism is the postcolonial problem of national identity. Previously expressed in rhetorical flourishes about "civilizing mission" and "White man's burden," the condition of national consciousness – "Britishness" and "Frenchness" were now examined more closely as domestic issues. Cultural expansiveness gave way to national introspection as the two former great imperialist powers lost what the French rather grandiloquently had called their "colonial vocation." The former American secretary of state Dean Acheson put the matter bluntly in a speech he gave in 1962: "Great Britain has lost an empire and has not yet found a role."

Perhaps defensive in the face of that condition of loss, leaders in both nations sought an adjustment to their previously certain national identity. The debate largely centered on the issue of plurality. Could a new multi-ethnic society "function harmoniously," as was claimed to be possible in the Swann Report of 1985 on education in Great Britain, by encouraging all ethnic groups to shape that society "within a framework of commonly accepted values, practices and procedures," while also allowing "distinct ethnic identities within that framework."[1]

The optimism of the authors of the Swann Report was countered by the pessimism of those who saw compounding negative conditions, who imagined something of a persistent, alien environmentalism that ill-suited the national situation. One representative at the 1972 Conservative Party Conference questioned whether a better decision concerning the fate of Ugandan Asian refugees would not have been for the government to have asked those Asian Commonwealth countries "where the language, the food, and the climate are familiar" to have accepted these people.[2] In a recent study of racism in France, a team of sociologists examined French attitudes toward the immigrants in several cities. One French female worker in Mulhouse is quoted as saying that residential immigrants from North Africa

> do not have the same attitudes as we do, don't have our laws or our values or our religion. They want to live as they did in their own country and all but impose their views on us. This is an impossible situation![3]

In a sweeping reversal the interwar debate over the "native problem" in the colonies seems to have become a contemporary debate over the immigrant problem in the former colonial metropolises. Struggling with a bothersome history and an unwanted legacy, the British and the French find decolonization as much a domestic as an overseas issue. In the several legislative acts on immigration that ran from the British Nationality Act of 1948 to the British Nationality Act of 1991, the debate against restriction centered on the Commonwealth as a multi-national, multi-ethnic institution of unique proportions. The home country accordingly had to practice what it so grandly proclaimed and therefore allow such immigration, it was argued by some. Those in opposition claimed that the restrictive policies practiced in some of the Commonwealth nations ought be allowed in Great Britain; or, further, that international law only required admission of one's nationals, which few of the Commonwealth citizens were.

As if in a grand swing of events, the colonial situation seems to have come full circle. Transplantation, which was the seventeenth- and eighteenth-century notion of building new communities with old institutions, such as New York and New Jersey, New France and New Zealand, in places that were declared "empty," has in the late twentieth century taken new form. Now, ethnic enclaves are situated in major European cities where people whose ancestors had existed under colonial rule must exist in a post-modern environment of urban decay, economic uncertainty, and social unrest. Decolonization has not yet occurred in the European metropolises because political decolonization overseas has transmitted and concentrated some of the worst aspects of the colonial situation to London and Paris – and to Los Angeles as well.

8 Land and language

Concerns over the perceived continuing European presence

The disappearance of formal empire did not mean the end of the colonial experience in the opinion of many critics. For them decolonization required much more: a fundamental change of outlook and attitude, of heart and mind. In an aptly chosen phrase, "bush clearing" was declared necessary.

This task was one that the first generation of postcolonial writers examined as they described and analyzed the postcolonial situation and often sought, through their writings, to help create a sense of "national consciousness," to use a term popular at the time. The word describing the condition against which this national consciousness was directed is the adjective "hegemonic" which bore the connotation of pervasive domination and control, the outside–in, top–down condition that all critics of cultural imperialism abhorred. The particularistic – the ideas, values, institutions, and environment that marked a culture off from others and that, conversely, guaranteed it a sense of collective identity – was praised, while the universalist, also considered the Eurocentric, that sought to obliterate such distinctions was denounced.

As the task of generating a sense of national consciousness was one of creating new patterns of thought and ways of seeing, the first postcolonial generation of writers and film makers developed a body of work that was largely social realist in approach and content, an examination of a landscape still contained within a European cultural context and of social and cultural attitudes that were derivatively European.

This peculiar condition, a sort of cultural alienation, is what the Kenyan author Ngugi wa Thiong'o described in *Decolonizing the Mind* (1989) as the double colonial alienation: the distancing of oneself from reality, and the identification with what is external to one's environment. According to his interpretation, what is seen and studied by the African is inauthentic, untrue to the local history and tradition of time and space and expressed in an idiom that can only distort what is being described. Imposed from without, the European order of land and language, like a palimpsest of old, overlaid and covered what was previously there, in this instance what is described as the precolonial culture or, in the stark words of the literary critic Lewis Nkosi, in his *Tasks and Masks* (1991), as the "smashed up cultures."

Such a condition was not unique to the postcolonial world, however. It had previously appeared in much of European literature where the old order of things was bruised, when not pushed aside, by the new, by the rush and the regulation of the modern. The English author Matthew Arnold, for instance, wrote of life "before this strange disease of modern life, with its sick hurry, its divided aims" in a poem he composed in 1854. In that same year, Charles Dickens' memorable criticism of the industrial city, the novel *Coketown*, appeared, with its description of a cityscape marked by the dismal sameness of soot-ridden brick buildings from which workers emerged in early morning, their bodies already bent by the heavy thought of the relentless routine daily imposed by the factory.

However, what made the postcolonial world distinctive was the double foreignness of the cultural condition it endured: change imposed from without and not generated within while justified – or rationalized – by values and attitudes that found no comfortable place in traditional indigenous thought. Moreover, this condition was compounded by the inequity, the condescension and often the contempt with which Europeans treated what they found and what they therefore thought they could easily replace, discard, or override.

A critical examination of this phenomenon of mental and cultural transplantation is what the currently popular academic subject "postcolonial discourse" is about. It is chiefly concerned with and suspicious of the formative power of language to create ideological conditions of domination, whether in a gender-empowering term like "mankind" or in a socially demeaning one like "native" or "boy." The idioms of speech accordingly not only reinforce social disparity but help define it. With the acute interest that Sherlock Holmes took in the dog that did not bark, contemporary critics are interested in what was not seen (the term is "hidden spaces") and what was not heard (the voice of the underling, the "subaltern").

These are matters of distinctiveness, of the particular and the local, that are lost in broad categorization and sweeping concept. As the South African novelist J. M. Coetzee has said in an essay in *White Writing* (1988), the literary expression of landscape must escape "the imperial gaze." There is no grand prospect, a high and removed assessment of all that lay spread out before the horizon. And so it might be said that there is nothing quaint or exotic except when falsely referenced to such sites of modernity as Trafalgar Square and the Champs Elysées. What Coetzee says of the South African landscape might more broadly be said of all: an intelligent reading of it demands on-the-knees, close-to-hand examination.

If there is one phrase that captures the mentality against which all such protests are lodged, it is the nineteenth-century maxim "lord of all he sees." Such was the dominating view of things shaped and structured by European or Western thought and practice that derived directly from notions of the superiority and universal applicability of European methods of thinking and doing, of "disciplinary" approaches, such as history, anthropology and sociology; and of on-site practices such as surveying, mapping, and, most prominent of all, land use. Framing and supporting all of this was a particular "master narrative," an assessment of modern history as the account of progress and betterment initiated in Europe and then spread around the world.

The imagined arrangement was but a variation of the old core–periphery argument of thought, ideas and observation radiating outward: what was first generated "here," in England and France, for instance, was then transported "there," to Egypt and Tahiti, for instance. The philosopher Etienne Gilson once remarked that the particular quality of the French was their intellectual pretension to universality. Gilson's remark, with some extension, sums up the mental attitude and the physical practices of the Europeans who sought to transfer and thus extend their own sense of space and place, of analysis and expression, "overseas."

Yet there is more to the matter. Such respatialization brought forth a "conflict of memories"[1] between those that grew out of the colonial experience and those that were denied by it. Memory is a function of space; the past is arranged by spatial referents, found in terms like "sacred ground" and "familiar sights." In reworking the physical space of the territories into which they moved so as to ensure and justify their own domination, as they did with forts and hospitals as well as with roads and railroads, the Europeans forced drastic changes in the local geography of the mind.

One of the most compelling expressions of this condition, simply and indirectly presented, is found on the first page of the autobiography of the Nigerian playwright Wole Soyinka. The work is entitled *Aké* (1981), the name of Soyinka's childhood home. Therein, on a Sunday, God is imagined to descend from the crest of a local mountain and to go directly to church in giant strides, after passing over the marketplace and bypassing the stables of the pagan chief. Instead of such possible stops,

God strode into St Peter's for morning service, paused briefly at the afternoon service, but reserved his most formal, exotic presence for the evening service which, in his honour, was always held in the English language.

The novels of the first generation of postcolonial writers are charged with concern over the effects of this sort of physical and social dislocation and fragmentation. Nevertheless, the anticipation of the new, purged of the colonial past and joining together society in a national consciousness that transcended the "divide and conquer" policy that had made imperialism workable, was quickly dashed. Instead of a new order of things, the new realities of civil strife and personal aggrandisement, of conflict and corruption, infused many of these social-realistic novels with a spirit of pessimism and cynicism. For many of the novelists, theirs was a world quickly marked by dissatisfaction and disillusion, a condition so obviously captured in the title of Chinua Achebe's second novel in his saga of the Okonkwo family, *No Longer at Ease*, taken from a T. S. Eliot poem which speaks of a similar condition. And that spirit is found, half a world away, in the Samoan Albert Wendt's novel, *Leaves of the Banyan Tree*, published a year before Soyinka's work and like it a family saga that traces generations of conflict, and adjustment to imposed modernity, to what is called "Other-Worlder pretense," charged with what the hero, Tauliopepe, once called in a sermon of hope, "God, money and success."

Postcolonial literature offers as one of its most complex and critically appraised works Salman Rushdie's *Midnight's Children*. Written in 1981 by the well-known Indian author who lives in England, this is a multilayered and comically interwoven story of two of those 1,001 children born at midnight on August 15, 1947, the hour when India received its independence. Switched at birth and mispaired in personality and social condition, the two young protagonists of the novel follow and encapsulate the first thirty years of India's existence. As Prime Minister Nehru is given to say in a letter he sends Saleem Sinai, one of the two children who is the narrator of the tale, "You're the newest bearer of that ancient face of India which is also eternally young." Then Nehru adds that Saleem's life will be "in a sense, the mirror of our own." And so the public history of the one is to be reflected in the individual life of the other: India and Saleem journey awkwardly, confusedly, and painfully through time, each bearing unpleasant marks of the experience. Rushdie, in a manner described as both surreal and magical, writes of that failed India, the new one that he saw as divided, as self-serving, and as cruel as the one which existed in the days of the Raj.

Such concerns expressed in the impressive body of postcolonial literature were further illuminated on the screen. Film makers in the era of decolonization described conflicting and altered patterns of landscape and space and the effect they had on the sense of self and place. Previously, in films made in Europe and the United States, Africa and Asia were depicted as broad, exotic, or forbidding landscapes, to which "natives" were added as another environmental element. The overhead and panoramic shots that provided sweep enhanced the wild romance of jungle-deep or desert-spanning mystery that such films sought to convey. This has been called the "Tarzanized" approach to such film making in which the Europeans are presented as action heroes. Its most successful counterpart, however, was the treatment of the colonial situation as comic in the so-called "road pictures" made by Bing Crosby and Bob Hope in the 1930s and 1940s. The "classic" of the set is the *Road to Morocco* (1942) in which Hope and Crosby are hapless innocents stumbling into and out of the mysterious, the exotic, and the amusing – at least as construed by Western audiences.

In such films Africa and Asia were backdrops in which the indigenous environment and its people were superficially fixed. As the Senegalese film director Ousmane Sembene remarked, "African landscapes were used as settings." Or, according to the Ethiopian cinematographer Haile Gerima, "Africans are part of the landscape."[2] Perhaps the last of that particular romantic genre of outdoor epic which so appealed to Western audiences was *Zulu*, a British production of 1964. However, in this film, the drama is of interaction, not domination, as African characters appear as strong in personality and will as do the English. More recently, the grand sweep of empire was entertained for the first time on television in a BBC series entitled *The Jewel in the Crown* (1984), based on the novels of Paul Scott, *The Raj Quartet*. Highly acclaimed, the series which depicted the last years of British rule in India has also been criticized as steeped in an atmosphere of nostalgia, with the trappings and settings of empire dramatically set out to embellish a plot concerned with the British, not the Indian, question: to what purpose all of this?

The postcolonial films produced in Africa and Asia usually sought to raise and answer smaller questions about matters of quite different dimensions. Accordingly, the geography was rescaled: crowded quarters and small enclosures dominated the urban scene where the conditions of poverty, unemployment and prostitution figured into plots concerned with the dichotomy between the traditional and the modern, the rural and the urban. Often stressing a social realism analogous to that found in the novels of the period, these films sought to visualize the distinctive and the particular, the trials and tribulations of "little people" caught up in a world of threatening dimensions.

Nowhere was this unsettled social condition more compellingly presented than in Indian cinema, one of the liveliest and most extensive in the immediate postcolonial era. While much of the Indian film industry rivalled Hollywood in the fantasy and escapist films that it turned out, the serious form of art film also emerged in which the problems of tradition and modernity, countryside and city, rich and poor were sensitively described. Of all the film makers who so examined the human condition, none has been more highly praised than Satyajit Ray, a Bengali, whose "Apu Trilogy," filmed in the 1950s, traces the journey of a boy into manhood and his personal journey from countryside to city. As Ray told one of his interviewers, all of his films are "concerned with the new versus the old."[3]

As did Ray with the Bengal region with which he was so familiar, so did several of the African film makers with their own settings. One of the earliest such efforts and one that has reached the status of film classic is Ousmane Sembene's film *Mandabi* (*The Money Order*, 1968) which poignantly captured the confining and overwhelming urban environment of Dakar as an old man sought to cash a money order sent from Paris, the particular object and its broader cultural context completely unknown, indeed baffling, to him.

However, many of the earlier postcolonial Asian films were unfavorably reviewed as being principally concerned with the validation of what has been called "national space." Moviemaking, generally a national industry often supported by state funds and directed to a large, national audience, thus tended to justify the nation state. Just as colonial films rose above the local and the proximate that were their focal points to the imperial that was their message, so many of the early films produced in the newly emerging nations were expressions of transcendent nationalism. The Indonesian film *The Jade Princess* (1964), it has been pointed out, opens with a panoramic shot of a group of Indonesians in diverse regional costumes, joined together in the singing of the national anthem.

Other films disassemble this "national space" by showing its distinct and often contradictory parts and conditions; they thus refute the "monological narrative of nationhood."[4] Such film situations have shown a radical view of things in which the nation state is represented as an imported and dominating construct serving the interest of a dominant bourgeoisie, much as the colonial state that had preceded it served the "topside" interests of the Europeans.

The emergence, largely from Latin America, of a Third World form of film criticism has recently reinforced this way of seeing things, of focusing the camera's lens and positioning the director's point of view. "Perfect" cinema, that of a commercial, audience-projected sort, so identified with Hollywood, is contrasted with "imperfect" cinema, in which the professional gives way to the participatory with film makers and audience often one and the same and with the purpose of finding its audience "in those who struggle."[5] Here is an expression of protest against a perceived neo-colonialism marked by elitism and cultural condescension that is joined with the intention of assuring a revolutionary perspective on the film so as to present "a throbbing living reality."[6]

A comparable position has been taken by a small group of Indian scholars who condemned the "hegemonic historiography" that they found distortive of the South Asian experience in the modern era. According to their appraisal, most of the history hitherto written about the independence movement in that part of the world was conceived either as a sort of challenge from and response to imperialism or as a series of accounts of the heroic role of leaders like Gandhi and Nehru in arousing popular resistance to British rule. This historiography was, in the words of Ranajit Guha, the guiding light of the new interpretation, "dominated by elitism – colonialist elitism and bourgeois-nationalist elitism." To engender a contrary mode of analysis Guha founded *Subaltern Studies* in 1982, a series of essays that has since become influential in offering a radical revisionism to what Guha called the "neo-colonialist and neo-nationalist form of discourse in Britain and India respectively."[7]

Such interpretations of the continuing effects of the colonial experience on the mind and over the land emphasized the concern raised by Africans and Asians over the perceived continuation of European domination.

With this concern, and perhaps even more intensely debated than it has been, is the matter of language and literature. Postcolonial discourse is a complicated subject. It is concerned with the formative and deformative power of language and the cultural conditions it obviously expresses and even imposes. Fanon was not the first to argue it, but he said it well in his *Black Skin, White Masks* (1952): "to speak a language is to assume a world, a culture."

Each European language as the local colonial vehicle of expression, whether Dutch in Sumatra, French in Senegal, Portuguese in Angola, assisted the colonial act, defined it, gave it a reality. Domination, it has been argued, was reinforced by cultural acquiescence, an acceptance of the imposing culture principally through its written word. There in road signs, newspaper headlines, police reports, and identity papers, the

European language controlled. In some sense its literature did as well. Fiction and analytical studies often followed or reworked European plots or constructs, answered colonialism in its own language with its own devices. Such literary efforts thus authenticated by use of European ideas, idioms, and plots the significance of the imperialist act. By "coming full circle," by turning the devices of imperialism on itself, the opponents suggested that imperialism somehow still held the ring, continued to define and embrace reality. To rework plot and situation of *The Tempest, Robinson Crusoe* or *Jane Eyre*, as has been done, was only to describe the colonial situation from a different perspective. The old core and periphery argument of imperialism seems even to persist here, although the direction of activity is reversed: the fiction is sent home as it were. (A collection of critical essays on the subject bears the title *The Empire Writes Back*, perhaps a double affirmation of the continuing cultural domination of the West, now also from Hollywood as it once was only from London.)

None of this matters so much politically and ideologically, however, as does the debate over European languages as vehicles of expression throughout Africa. Without a far-backward-reaching written literary tradition, although endowed with one of the world's richest oral traditions, contemporary Africans have engaged in an often acrimonious debate over the effect of writing in the imposed language, in English in particular. Chinua Achebe, perhaps the most renowned of African authors, has defended the use of English, contending that he has adapted the language, has made it serve African interests and concerns. "But it will have to be a new English, still in full communion with its ancestral home but altered to suit new African surroundings," he contended in his essay, "The African Writer and the English Language" (1965).

In opposition to this argument stands Ngugi wa Thiong'o, the Kenyan novelist. In what he announced was his last work in English, Ngugi, who had already begun to write his novels in Gikuyu, wrote *Decolonizing the Mind*, originally a series of lectures delivered in New Zealand. The work is a strong denunciation of imperialism in its multiple forms, political, economic, and, above all, linguistic. Contending that the language used and the purposes to which it is directed define a people and their culture, Ngugi argues that Africans ought to recognize that writing in European languages is tacit acceptance of a form of neo-colonialism. In using these languages, "are we not paying homage to them, are we not on the cultural level continuing that neo-colonial slavish and cringing spirit?" There is more; it concerns centrality, what Ngugi says is a core–periphery issue: from what position does one look out at the world? Use of the English language joined with the study of English literature has created a reference system in which Africa is compared to Europe, not the other way around. Reform in the Kenyan schools, he notes with relief, has meant that African students no longer need to "detect Jane Austen's characters in their villages."

Since Ngugi delivered his lectures in 1984, the dominance of English in global discourse has been the source of a lively debate. No language is more regularly heard, whether in airports, on television, or in print, than English. In the fashion of the day where capitalized initials starkly stand for new concepts and new institutions, EIL has appeared as a popular acronym. English as the international language is both a statement of fact and a source of intense debate. Whether English is now spoken well by 400 million persons or poorly by upwards of 2 billion is of less consequence than what this dominance of that language has come to mean.

Arguably the most lively of the postcolonial intellectual debates is over the history of the English language as a weapon of domination and control. The origin of the debate is found in post-modernism. The literary theory that "discourse" is concerned with narrative was expressive of values, culture, social conditions, and – above all – ideology. English is thus more than linguistically dominant: it is not a simple vehicle of communication but rather is trucked in as heavy ideological freight. The political significance of this theory of language has gained in intensity as the contemporary world has been so shaped and defined by this language. It is the expression of commerce and science, of international airline pilot conversation, of reference systems, such as libraries and the Internet; of international diplomacy, and of electronic entertainment, whether through the recordings of the Beatles and Elvis Presley or television shows such as *Dallas* and the output of CNN (Cable News Network). So widespread is this language usage that some analysts argue for a lower-cased noun, "english," to distinguish its status as a sort of lingua franca and to degeographize it and thus ensure that it is no longer mistakenly identified with the mind-set of once Merrie England.

The globalization of English begs the question: what caused it? Was its usage initially a device of imperialism to ensure control, or did it spread as do epidemics, more slowly than influenza, of course, but with comparably deadly effect? The latter is the more easily answered question and so will be addressed first. A stage theory has been proposed which traces English over a broad sweep of history: first, with its transplantation to the New World with the colonists; then with its extension, notably in the late nineteenth century, to areas of European domination and trade where non-native speakers acquired use of the language; and, finally, to the contemporary situation where telecommunications (television and transistor radio) have replaced maritime trade (bills of lading and custom receipts), and English enters the home as conveyor of entertainment as well as the market place where it is the literary medium of the majority of software.

The answer to the first question posed above is more controversial because it more clearly involves the question of intent. Historically, the answer reaches back to British policy in India and particularly to the minute prepared by Thomas Babington Macaulay in 1835 in which he urged English instruction for an elite which would assist in imperial control. While its effects are now considered to have been exaggerated, Macaulay's minute is widely accepted as the first statement that defined the relationship of language and imperialism. Whether that relationship was structured to become an instrument of colonial policy is now part of the debate, one group seeing a conscious effort on the part of the British to spread the language as a means of political control and others who see the development as neither coordinated nor holistic but more haphazard and simply responsive to perceived local needs.

More significant was English's "indirect rule," its worldwide insinuation not so much as colonial governmental policy as an attendant condition of the development of capitalism and regional markets. Rather as Swahili had grown to become the trading language of the East African coast in the eighteenth and nineteenth centuries, English became the language of international commerce, a condition resulting first from British and then American economic supremacy.

In our own time the global dominance of the United States in popular culture – television series and fast-food restaurants, most obviously – allows the argument of the existence of a new cultural imperialism, more pernicious than the old because more subtly dominant than previously. Only recently, the Iraqi government denounced the Internet as a tool of American imperialism and therefore has forbidden its use in that country. Less draconian, but still made in the direction of governmental control, have been the efforts in China and Singapore to limit access to the Internet. In an article appearing in the *New York Times* (April 14, 1996), Anatoly Voronov, director of Glastnet, the major Russian-language internet, spoke of the Worldwide Web as "the ultimate act of intellectual colonialism." The English language is the new currency of exchange, with the result that the world is now made "into new sorts of haves and have nots."

The issue, however, is more complex than Voronov and other like-minded critics allow. If English has gained a prominence in the contemporary world that shades all other languages, it stands as no single standard bearer. Indeed, there are those who argue that the most lively and innovative literary expression of English comes from the country in which Macaulay first imposed it as a means of imperial control, India. In an article in the *New Yorker* (June 23, 1997) celebrating the fiftieth anniversary of Indian independence and the rich literature that has followed, Salman Rushdie offered this strong conclusion: "'Indo-Anglian' literature represents perhaps the most valuable contribution India has yet made to the world of books." Not only in India itself but scattered around the world, in a sort of self-generated diaspora, Indian writers, critics, academics, and film makers have made English a vehicle of contemporary criticism and insight that knows no national boundaries and that arises from no single soil.

Such a condition does not, however, allay particular fears of language dominance – and the apparent threats to that condition. In the United States, where over 300 languages are now spoken, moves have been under way to legalize English as the national language. The states of California and Arkansas have, for instance, enacted legislation to that effect by making English the official language. These actions were taken in light of Mexican immigration and the consequent spread of Spanish as the vernacular language in the southern tier of the United States. In the French-speaking world, a strong movement to strengthen "francophonia," the expression of French language and culture, has led to a variety of activities, including ministerial conferences, the creation of the International Association of French Speaking Parliamentarians and the inauguration of the Franocophone Games, the first held in Morocco in 1989 with representatives of thirty-nine nations in attendance (and, no doubt, with players and referees arguing in French). Most recently, the former secretary-general of the United Nations, Boutros Boutros-Ghali, has become secretary-general of the blanket French-language organization, *La Francophonie*, some indication of the seriousness of the matter.

Such efforts to reinforce a cultural position, to defend a language, to ensure that space conforms to historical expectations are neither new nor unusual. What distinguishes the concerns over space and language in the postcolonial age is twofold: scale and intensity. The global age in which no major city is more than a day's air travel from any other, and in which all airplanes and all airports are without discernible variation, suggests the first time in human history when the word "foreign" has lost most of its meaning (and has, in fact, been banned from usage on the Cable News Network). The intensity of communications, as marked by the Internet and Worldwide Web has certainly given the

English language a precedence unmatched by any other at any other time. While still intensely argued in academic circles, particularly those found in Western Europe and the United States, the issue of "decolonizing the mind," the all-encapsulating phrase of Ngugi wa Thiong'o, has now subsided as a subject of popular debate and interest in what was once the postcolonial world. Colonialism and its aftermath are largely historical subjects today. Two generations have grown up since the contemporaries of Nehru and Senghor rejoiced with them over independence. During that time, communism as a world-shaping force declined and disappeared. Everywhere, capitalism seems to be embraced and market-driven economics favored. As a professor at the University of Dar es Salaam recently said of the university's shift from academic concerns with *ujaama*, Nyerere's expression of a new social collectivity, to concerns of a market economy, "Today people are more concerned about their welfare than ideology."

9 Beyond empire

Current issues and conditions in the study of imperialism and decolonization

The last decade of the twentieth century is the first in two millennia without a significant empire. Japan alone among major states bears the title, but nothing more. The last of those vast political enterprises held in place by military force, not popular agreement, was that dominated by the Soviet Union whose disintegration was dramatically marked with the fall of the Berlin Wall in 1989. Since then, empire is only used as a meaningful qualifier for the telecommunications industry, the domain of which is not geographically fixed in a traditional sense: air waves and cyberspace have no ports of entry or discernible frontiers.

The major issues centering on the hard reality of imperialism have been resolved, discarded or overwhelmed by others. Who bothers to look at the statue of Hubert Lyautey, France's most celebrated pro-consul, as it stands in Paris devoid of the landscape features of ceremony: flower beds and benches? Who among the annual number of Rhodes Scholars knows of or cares about the big plans of the little man who endowed those scholarships to build a Cape-to-Cairo railroad? The memorials to such men, like the monumental efforts they made to ensure the greatness and endurance of empire, attract little attention. Only the marketable romance of wicker furniture, khaki shorts, gin, and the Raffles Hotel in Singapore reminds us that the banner of the London *Daily Mail* was once timely: "For Queen and Empire."

Yet, at first blush, the West seems not to have relinquished its dominant position in global affairs these several decades since the imperial retreat and the consequent jubilation of independence. As was already said at that time, the Coca-Cola-ization of the world is assured, and now even more widely regnant is Microsoft computer software, upon which 90 per cent of the world's computers currently run. Add automobile and aircraft production, steel and chemical production, even the output of companies making sports shoes and compact disks to these obvious indicators, and it is obvious that the handful of highly industrialized

nations with postmodern telecommunications industries have now com-
modified the world as it once had been imperialized. No indicators of
this condition are more evident than the number of videocassette rental
stores on the Fiji Islands or shops in the Caribbean tour ships' ports-of-
call selling Japanese cameras.

What lies in thought and mentality behind such commodification is
the broad subject of one of the liveliest of current academic debates. It
particularly concerns power, in the form of dominance, as expressed in
space and sign. It therefore centers on communication, both the silent
statements of spatial configurations and the stated ones in master narratives and local stories. The scholarly examination of these
configurations is new, the interest first expressed some two decades ago
by the "deconstructionists" who found behind and beneath every text
an ideology and in every narrative an expression of power. To speak or
write is to command, to organize a universe of sorts. There is therefore
no condition of authorial objectivity, they would argue.

If this academic contention is quite new, the historical matter it has
examined is quite old. It has been dated at that early moment when
Columbus first made entries in his journals in which the landscape he
saw, not the people he encountered, was described. Then, shortly thereafter, when he did turn his attention to the local population, what he
saw and described was their nakedness. Columbus was thus the first to
denude of their humanity those people who were victims of European
conquest.[1] Europeans thereafter constructed a global narrative in which
all that was "overseas," "on the other shore," gained historical significance only in its newly established relationship with the intruders who
had telescopes and could write, who could therefore focus on what they
considered important and account for it as they wished. The Europeans
then began to manage the world.

However, some new critics argue that this historical development was
not unidirectional; it was not simply the definition of one by another or,
in the current lexicon, of the Other by the European. In the encounter
with the people they colonized, the Europeans began to define themselves by the contrasts they found and imagined to be. They created a
special cultural dependency relationship; their vaunted superiority
required a juxtaposed inferiority: the "civilized" required the existence
of the "uncivilized." As one anthropologist has put it: "[It] was through
the study and narrativization of colonial others that Europe's history
and culture could be celebrated as unique and triumphant."[2]

Such external appraisal, in which the imagined cultural linearity that
was proudly called the line of progress by nineteenth-century
Europeans, was also accompanied in popular European thought, or so

have argued some postcolonial critics, by a general and usually unquestioning acceptance of European domination, an attitude so widespread as to need no special comment. Such was the case in many of the novels written in the nineteenth and early twentieth centuries. So frequently were narratives foregrounded against such colonial circumstance that the literary critic Edward Said has been led to say: "Without empire . . . there is no European novel as we now know it."[3] Consider only the children's story *The Secret Garden* (1909), by Frances Hodgson Burnett, the plot of which is propelled into being by a cholera outburst in Bombay which kills the heroine's parents and thus forces her to go to England to live with an uncle, an experience doubly alien to the young girl.

The familiarity of empire in literature was matched by a general cultural familiarity as well. In drawing up any inventory of thoughts, customs, and commodities imported from overseas, the historian must acknowledge that Frantz Fanon was not altogether incorrect in saying that Europe was a creation of the Third World. There were, among other colonial imports, afternoon tea, the bungalow, and pajamas. And it is not going too far to say that even interior decorating for the well off and high born was influenced by the colonial scene. The most obvious – and perhaps the most grotesque – example may be the preserved elephant foot serving as an umbrella rack, a quintessential touch of domestic exoticism and an in-house statement about command of the world.

Space was the conditioner of imperialist thought and attitudes. It was there in expressions of geographical distinction, like "far away," the "Near East," "Darkest Africa"; and in expressions concerning human patterns of existence, like "teeming masses," "yellow hordes," "naked savages." It was soon there in the photograph and the movie, in which indigenous peoples were posed, configured as elements in an environment that stood before the viewer, which he or she could thus closely examine – but at a comfortable social distance. Imperialism, then, was a way of seeing things, of arranging space.

This arrangement has been intensely analyzed as an expression of space-as-power. Particularly since the seminal works of the French scholar Michel Foucault, whose *Discipline and Punish* (1977) is especially notable, the various modes of power available to state and society by which to effect control of individuals and groups have been subjects of keen interest. Recent students of decolonization have also considered the matter and have analyzed spatial arrangements as the means by which the colonial authorities were able to maintain and indeed expand their authority.

Even before these analyses, colonial officers "in the field" exercised such notions and put them into practice. The French colonial officer Joseph Gallieni admonished in 1892, as he was commanding the military conquest of Tonkin in French Indochina, "build in durable materials," construct forts in concrete so that the local population knows the French have enduring intentions. Something of that "seating" of power was done on a grand scale with the lay-out and construction of New Delhi as imperial capital in the early twentieth century, as it was in a lesser but more appealing manner in Rabat, the administrative capital of French Morocco. And in a somewhat different sense, the ethnographic museum, with its neatly labeled and glass-encased exhibits, and with its arrangements made according to European-determined concepts of place or time, was an affirmation of the colonial power to arrange space.[4] Like the photograph, the exhibition of artifacts and the diorama of "native life" invited the observer to view what had been arranged and contrived for a purpose that was completely removed from the cultural context of the person or persons who formed the subject.

Postcolonial analysis, however, now finds cultural situations not quite so tidy as they were depicted in museum exhibits, photographs, or international colonial expositions. Space, language, and the cultures they define are mixed up, rudely blended together. The term "hybridization," first applied to organic growth, has now been translated to cultural development.[5] It serves well as a term descriptive of the post-colonial world, in which what was once imposed has now been appropriated, where land and language have acquired different dimensions and relationships now that the Europeans have moved out and the formerly colonized can move about and speak their own minds. A complementary term describing such hybridization is an easily appreciated one: "creolization."

Perhaps, then, the lasting effect of the imperialist experience is to be ethnically diverse, spatio-linguistically diverse communities, and a dominating language, so infused by new idioms and pronunciations as to defy further identification as the "Queen's English." Rather, it will become the language of a new literary cosmopolitanism, with works composed by what Salman Rushdie has called "mongrel" personalities, authors of diverse cultural backgrounds writing in a language which is not their native tongue. In this sense, decolonization that was initially a matter of the transfer of power from empire to nation state has been succeeded by a postcolonial culture that is a blend or mix that belies the sharp distinctions symbolically announced by the three different colors that usually make up a national flag.

Changes in local cuisine suggest this condition most pungently. What major community, whether Vienna or Vancouver, does not boast of an outstanding Chinese or Indonesian restaurant, does not frequently offer couscous or rice as the part of a main dish once triumphantly occupied by potatoes, does not quickly provide falafel pocket sandwiches to those in a hurry, Australian wine and Chinese beer to those who wish to linger?

What may thus pass as international charm, a cosmopolitanism more authentic than that found in Disneyworld, should not be allowed to deflect concern away from the fundamental failures accompanying what was originally intended to be a political and economic process, "decolonization."

"The most fundamental aspect of post-independence Africa has been the elusiveness of development," wrote the historian J. F. Ade Ajayi in 1982.[6] His words need not be changed today in an analysis of much of the former colonial world. Latin America, the Caribbean, Southeast Asia, and the Middle East join Africa as regions marked by places of despair and desperation, of those ecologies where shattered dreams are found in cracked foundations and high hopes cannot be seen behind the huge piles of garbage. The genocide of the last few years in Rwanda, the religious unrest and violent encounter of rival groups in Algeria, the need to hire South African mercenary soldiers to bring a modicum of peace to Sierra Leone, ruthless dictatorship in Iraq and religious intolerance in Iran, child prostitution in the Philippines and abject poverty in Burkina Faso, all weigh heavily. How unfortunate it seemed that the prime minister of India in his speech celebrating that nation's fiftieth anniversary of independence was compelled to threaten: "Some people think that corruption is their birthright. I am warning them."

The general postcolonial situation continues to be grim for much of the world. Its relief also seems at best uncertain. A new bifurcation of the world now exists, not in the traditional geometry of core and periphery, but rather as a sharp, horizontal linearity. A handful of wealthy nations running east–west from Japan and Korea to the United States and on to Western Europe stand economically above (as they do figuratively on a Mercator-projection map) those mostly found below the equator, where poverty seems endemic and economic stagnation a condition of place, of ecological disadvantage.

There is no certainty in global analysis these days. The imagined lines of simple division in the nineteenth century, so comforting to the then dominant Europeans, are all gone. There is no longer any "home" and "abroad," any "east" and "west," any "core" and "periphery." Even "foreign" and "familiar" have become fuzzy terms, as evidenced in the instructions for any electronic instrument, say a Japanese video player, that are printed in at least three languages; and as the universal success of tourism proves, with its international hotel chains and airlines assuring the traveler that all differences will be only superficially exotic.

Imperialism and colonialism, attitudes of arrogance mobilized into doctrines of need and deed, markets and morality, have changed the world. There is no way to unchange that; history allows no going back. Accordingly, there is little likelihood that efforts to find an anterior authentic voice and a distinct historic identity will prevail in the Third World. Whether described as hybrid or multi-ethnic, whether found in London or Kuala Lumpur, whether expressed in English or Gikuyu, the matter is necessarily of a contemporary blend. Edward Said, therefore, urges a "contrapuntal" approach to examination of the nature and effects of empire and does so by alluding to the contrapuntal in Western music, where "various themes play off one another."[7] There should therefore be admitted various readings, different voices, other perspectives. Juxtaposed, if not complemented, these expressions of the human condition might allow a rich and balanced appreciation of what occurred and of what might yet become.

Forster's concluding narrative line in his novel *A Passage to India* voiced that hope of conjunction of peoples and cultures. The conditions described at that point in the novel seemed to say to the narrator, "'No, not yet,' and the sky said, 'No, not there'." The "there," that earlier set of spatial and cultural configurations established by modern imperialism, is largely gone. Whatever the future appearance of the world, it certainly will offer no reflection of that particular past.

Chronology of political decolonization

Decolonization is most easily appreciated and measured as a series of political acts, occasionally peaceful, often confrontational, and frequently militant, by which territories and countries dominated by Europeans gained their independence. The expression "national liberation front" was widely used to describe the position assumed by those opposing colonial rule.

As the following chronology demonstrates, political decolonization forms a neat half-century time span, from the independence of India in 1947 to the return of Hong Kong to China in 1997. Lord Mountbatten represented the British at the first transfer of power; Prince Charles was in attendance at the second. (During part of the ceremonies, both men wore colonial whites, some expression of uniformity over the years.) If thus seemingly marked by British activity, the phenomenon was international and global, leading to the end of the 500-year historical span of European expansion and empire-building. Yet a close examination of the dates of independence reveals three major clusterings: in the late 1940s, national success was achieved in much of Southeast Asia; in the 1950s, North Africa took its turn. Then in the 1960s, the quickest, most intensive decolonization occurred in Sub-Saharan Africa where twenty-four republics then emerged.

It might be asserted that these clusters were the final realization of the argument made in the eighteenth century by the French philosopher Turgot that colonies, like fruit, would fall from the tree when ripe. In terms of his metaphor, the growing season (state of political organization and resistance) was more advanced in Southeast Asia, less so in Sub-Saharan Africa.

The chronology that follows, arranged by decades, is of the dates of independence of the principal colonies and colonial territories, with their new names in parantheses.

THE 1940s

1946	Philippines
1947	India and Pakistan [separated from India]
1948	Ceylon (Sri Lanka), Burma (Myanmar)
1949	Indonesia

THE 1950s

1951	Libya
1954	Vietnam, Cambodia, Laos [all formerly components of French Indochina]
1956	Egypt, Morocco
1957	Tunisia, Gold Coast (Ghana), Malaya (subsequently Federation of Malaysia when joined with Sarawak and Northern Borneo in 1963)
1958	Guinea

THE 1960s

1960	Senegal, Ivory Coast, Mauretania, French Sudan (Mali), Dahomey (Benin), Upper Volta (Burkina Faso) [all emerging from the French West African Federation]; Chad, Gabon, Central African Republic, Congo Republic [all emerging from the French Equatorial Federation]; Madagascar, Nigeria, Republic of Congo (later Zaire, now Democratic Republic of the Congo), Cyprus
1961	Republic of South Africa, Sierra Leone, Tanganyika (Tanzania when united with Zanzibar in 1964)
1962	Algeria, Uganda, Trinidad and Tobago, Jamaica
1963	Singapore (as part of the Federation of Malaysia, but a separate state since 1965), Kenya
1964	Nyasaland (Malawi), Northern Rhodesia (Zambia), Malta
1965	Rhodesia (Zimbabwe in 1979), Kenya, Maldives
1966	Bechuanaland (Botswana), Barbados, British Guiana (Guyana)
1968	Swaziland, Mauritius

THE 1970s

1970	Fiji, Tonga
1973	Bahamas

1974   Grenada
1975   Angola, Mozambique, Guinea-Bissau, Papua New Guinea
1976   Seychelles

THE 1980s

1981   Belize (formerly British Honduras), Antigua and Barbuda
1984   Brunei

THE 1990s

1994   Southwest Africa (Namibia)
1997   Hong Kong (handed over by British to China after ninety-nine
year lease)

Notes

In an effort to reduce notes to a minimum in this general introduction to the subject, references to major works directly cited are made in the text itself and are followed by the year of original publication. The notes are therefore chiefly restricted to works offering a distinctive argument that has been incorporated into the text and to remarks of an unusual nature that were found cited in interpretive studies.

1 IN THE AFTERNOON

1 The term is that of Mary Louise Pratt, *Imperial Eyes*, London, Routledge, 1992, p. 15.
2 See Edward Said, *Culture and Imperialism*, New York, Vintage, 1994, pp. 58–9.
3 Cited in Pierre Ryckmans, *Dominer pour servir,* Brussels, Universelle, 1948, p. 180.
4 Quoted in Albert Sarraut, *La Mise en valeur des colonies françaises*, Paris, Payot, 1923, p. 15.

2 THE SEA CHANGE OF EMPIRE

1 Quoted in Elliott Roosevelt, *As I Saw It*, New York, Duell, Sloan and Pearce, 1946, p. 115.
2 Quoted in William Roger Louis and Ronald Robinson, "The United States and the Liquidation of British Empire in Tropical Africa," in Prosser Gifford and William Roger Louis (eds), *The Transfer of Power in Africa*, New Haven, Yale University Press, 1982, p. 34. The general argument that immediately precedes the quotation in the text is largely derived from this article.
3 Quoted in Peter Wesley Smith, *Unequal Treaty*, Hong Kong, Oxford University Press, 1980, p. 163.
4 Quoted in Louis and Robinson, "The United States," p. 37.

3 INSTABILITY AND UNCERTAINTY

1 This tripartite division seems first to have been suggested by Louis and Robinson, "The United States," pp. 53–5.

4 PRONOUNCEMENTS, DENUNCIATIONS, AND THE SEARCH FOR IDEOLOGY

1 Quoted in Francoise Pfaff, *The Cinema of Ousmane Sembene*, Westport, Greenwood Press, 1984, p. 11.
2 See Hollis R. Lynch, "Pan-African Responses in the United States to British Colonial Rule in Africa in the 1940s," in Gifford and Louis (eds), *Transfer*, pp. 81–2.
3 See A. W. Singham and Shirley Hune, *Non-alignment in an Age of Alignments*, Westport, Lawrence and Hill, 1986, pp. 83–4.

5 COUNTRYSIDE AND CITY

1 See David Siddle and Kenneth Swindell, *Rural Change in Tropical Africa*, London, Basil Blackwell, 1990, chapter 7.
2 The photograph is found in George MacDonald Fraser, *The Hollywood History of the World*, New York, William Morrow, 1988, p. 141.
3 On this subject see the remarkable work of Jennifer Robinson, *The Power of Apartheid*, Oxford, Butterworth-Heinemann, 1996, notably chapter 2, the interpretation of which has been included in the narrative of this chapter.
4 Robinson, *The Power of Apartheid*, p. 205.
5 See Terence Ranger, "The Invention of Tradition in Colonial Africa," in Eric Hobsbawm and Terence Ranger (eds), *The Invention of Tradition*, Cambridge, Cambridge University Press, 1995.

6 "GOTTA BE THIS OR THAT"

1 See John W. Harbeson, "Military Rulers in African Politics," in John W. Harbeson (ed.), *The Military in African Politics*, New York, Praeger, 1987.

7 OUTSIDE IN

1 Quoted in Harry Gouldbourne, *Ethnicity and Nationalism in Post-Imperial Britain*, Cambridge, Cambridge University Press, 1991, p. 31.
2 Quoted in ibid., p. 117.
3 Quoted in Michel Wieviorka, *La France raciste*, Paris, Editions du Seuil, 1992, p. 10.

8 LAND AND LANGUAGE

1 V. Y. Mudimbe, *The Idea of Africa*, Bloomington, Indiana University Press, 1994, p. 140.

2 Both quoted in Pfaff, *Cinema*, pp. 3 and 9.
3 From an interview with Marie Seton, quoted in Marie Seton, *Satyajit Ray: Portrait of a Director*, Bloomington, Indiana University Press, 1971, p. 143.
4 Wimal Dissanayake, "Introduction," in Wimal Dissanayake (ed.), *Colonialism and Nationalism in Asian Cinema*, Bloomington, Indiana University Press, 1994, p. xxvi.
5 Quoted in Roy Armes, *Third World Film Making and the West* Berkeley, University of California Press, 1987, p. 98. The argument in the text is largely derived from Armes' incisive interpretation.
6 Ibid., p. 99.
7 Ranajit Guha, "On Some Aspects of the Historiography of Colonial India," in Ranajit Guha and Gayatri Chakravorty Spivak (eds), *Selected Subaltern Studies*, New York, Oxford University Press, 1988, p. 32.

9 BEYOND EMPIRE

1 See Tzvetan Todorov, *The Conquest of America: The Question of the Other*, trans., Richard Howard, New York, Harper and Row, 1982, pp. 34–5.
2 Nicholas B. Dirks, "Introduction: Colonialism and Culture," in Nicholas B. Dirks (ed.), *Colonialism and Culture*, Ann Arbor, University of Michigan Press, 1989, p. 6.
3 See Said, *Culture and Imperialism*, 69.
4 On this subject, see Mudimbe, *The Idea of Africa*, pp. 60–1.
5 On this development, see Robert J. C. Young, *Colonial Desire: Hybridity in Theory, Culture and Race*, London, Routledge, 1996, especially chapter 1.
6 Quoted in Neil Lazarus, *Resistance in Postcolonial Fiction*, New Haven, Yale University Press, 1990, p. 4.
7 Said, *Culture and Imperialism*, p. 51.

Annotated bibliography

Aldrich, Robert, *Greater France: A History of French Overseas Expansion*, New York, St. Martin's Press, 1996.

The most recent and most handy general account of the French colonial empire from its early inception until its recent conclusion. The section on decolonization is not extensive but provides a good political summary.

Ansprenger, Franz, *The Dissolution of the Colonial Empires*, London, Routledge, 1989.

One of the most recent general studies of decolonization, but including a general survey of empire in the twentieth century. Arranged by imperial power and its colonies, the text nevertheless gains some cohesion through the general contention that the British led the movement to decolonization. The text has aged prematurely as a result of the flood of new studies approaching the problem with post-modernist interpretations.

Armes, Roy, *Third World Film Making and the West*, Berkeley, University of California Press, 1987.

An analytical and well-written survey of film making that includes the decolonizing world and assesses the significance of the film as a popular instrument of ideology and cultural beliefs.

Ashcroft, Bill, Griffiths, Gareth, and Tiffin, Helen, *The Empire Writes Back: Theory and Practice in Post-colonial Literatures*, London, Routledge, 1989.

A very fine introduction to this broad subject, this book is as good a place to begin understanding the subject as can be found.

Betts, Raymond F., *France and Decolonisation, 1900–1960*, London, Macmillan, 1991.

A brief survey of the major conditions and developments of French colonization, with the text arranged by period, not by geographical area.

Bhagwati, Jadish, *India in Transition: Freeing the Economy*, London, Clarendon Press, 1993.

A most readable and clear account of the problems of India's economy by a well-known economist favoring a free-market system.

Bienen, Henry S., *Armed Forces, Conflict, and Change in Africa*, Boulder, Westview Press, 1989.

A most useful survey of the role of armed forces in decolonized Africa, with a particularly valuable chapter on the armed forces and modernization.

Clapham, Christopher, *Third World Politics*, Beckenham, Croom Helm, 1985.

A very concise and readable assessment of the principal political and economic concerns attending the emergence of the newly decolonized states.

Darby, Phillip, *Three Faces of Imperialism: British and American Approaches to Asia and Africa, 1870-1970*, New Haven, Yale University Press, 1987.

The three faces are the political ("power"), economic ("economic interests"), and cultural ("moral responsibility") motivations and justifications of modern imperialism and its conclusion. The book provides an effective assessment of the rise of American global domination and the decline of the British.

Darwin, John, *The End of Empire: The Historical Debate*, London, Basil Blackwell, 1991.

A well-knit and clearly presented assessment of the elements in the debate over British decolonization, this is an exceptionally useful book.

Dirks, Nicholas B. (ed.), *Colonialism and Culture,* Ann Arbor, University of Michigan Press, 1992.

These essays are expressive of the new, post-modernist interpretations of colonialism and demonstrate the range of interest in the subject.

Esedebes, P. Olisanwuche, *Pan-Africanism: The Idea and the Movement, 1776-1963*, Washington, Howard University Press, 1982.

A very fine survey, highly sympathetic to the movement, but carefully structured. The role of Pan-Africanism between World War II and African independence is well presented.

Freund, Bill, *The Making of Contemporary Africa: The Development of African Society since 1800*, Bloomington, Indiana University Press, 1984.

A very fine analysis, stressing cultural change and the reordering of African society in the last century. The chapters on decolonization are particularly good.

Godlewska, Anne and Smith, Neil, *Geography and Empire*, Oxford, Blackwell, 1994.

Although spread across time and place, this set of essays offers a good introduction to contemporary geographic thought on the subject of colonial empire. The essay by Jonathan Crush, "Post-colonialism, De-colonization, and Geography," is a very insightful analysis.

Gordon, Lewis R., *Fanon and the Crisis of European Man*, London, Routledge, 1995.

There are several good biographies of Frantz Fanon, one of the central figures in the debate over decolonization. This one concentrates on Fanon's thought and allows the reader to appreciate the significance of Fanon.

Gifford, Prosser and Louis, William Roger (eds), *The Transfer of Power in Africa: Decolonization 1940–1960*, New Haven, Yale University Press, 1982.

This is one of the finest collections of essays on the political aspects of decolonization. Written by outstanding scholars, the work is primarily arranged geographically.

Guha, Ranajit and Spivak, Gayatri Chakravorty, *Selected Subaltern Studies*, New York, Oxford University Press, 1988.

A most informative selection of articles from this significant publication, the book allows the reader to appreciate the opposition to "hegemonic historiography," here considered a legacy of imperialism in the postcolonial era.

Harbeson, John W. (ed.), *The Military in African Politics*, New York, Praeger, 1987.

A series of essay on particular military regimes in Africa, their origins and effectiveness.

James, Lawrence, *Imperial Rearguard: Wars of Empire, 1919-1985*, London, Brassey's Defence Publishers, 1988.

A narrative sympathetic to the subject it considers – the men who fought these wars – only makes this book all the more interesting.

Kiernan, V. G., *From Conquest to Collapse: European Empires, 1815-1960*, New York, Pantheon, 1982.

Critical of the entire venture, and emphasizing its capitalist exploitative nature, Kiernan provides the reader with a good and well-written overview.

Langley, J. Ayo, *Ideologies of Liberation in Black Africa, 1856–1970*, London, Rex Collings, 1979.

A rather magisterial collection of documents on the subject, this anthology is presented most sympathetically. No other volume contains so many speeches that are rather hard for the general student to find.

Louis, William Roger, *Imperialism at Bay: The United States and the Decolonization of the British Empire, 1941-1945*, New York, Oxford University Press, 1978.

This is a remarkably well-researched and detailed account of the intriguing wartime politics in the British empire and its postwar fate.

Low, D. A., *Eclipse of Empire*, Cambridge, Cambridge University Press, 1991.

A splendid set of essays, covering a variety of subjects that help give a composite picture of the end of the British empire.

Mudimbe, V. Y., *The Idea of Africa*, Bloomington, Indiana University Press, 1994.

A trenchant argument from a strong ideological perspective that suggests African culture has been distorted and twisted by Westerners, notably by anthropology which is seen as in service to colonialism. The book is a powerful and tightly argued indictment.

Newman, Judie, *The Ballistic Bard: Postcolonial Fictions*, London, Arnold, 1994.

A compelling analysis of some of the most significant postcolonial fiction in English, this book serves as a fine introduction to the subject.

Ngosi, Lewis, *Tasks and Mask: Themes and Style of African Literature*, Harlow, Longman, 1981.

A fine introduction to the issues surrounding the development of contemporary African literature and its expression in English.

Ngugi wa Thiong'o, *Decolonizing the Mind: The Politics of Language in African Literature*, London, James Currey, 1986.

These essays are written in controlled anger expressed against imperialism and the intellectual constructs and language that it has imposed on Africans. The author, a well-known Kenyan novelist, seeks an African literature expressed in an African idiom.

Parnwell, Mike, *Population Movements and the Third World*, London, Routledge, 1993.

A concise introduction to and explanation of the causes, nature, and scope of this major postwar phenomenon.

Pennycook, Alistair, *The Cultural Politics of English as an International Language*, London, Longman, 1994.

Of the several volumes recently published on the subject, this is perhaps the least contestual and the most balanced in historical development.

Potter, Robert B. and Sala, Ademola T., *Cities and Development in the Third World*, London, Mansell, 1990.

A series of essays on various urban problems as found in particular cities in the Third World. The introductory essay provides a meaningful framework upon which to study this phenomenon.

Pratt, Mary Louise, *Imperial Eyes, Travel Writing and Transculturation*, London, Routledge, 1992.

Although not concerned with decolonization, this book, one of the most significant concerned with European attitudes and cultural biases, provides an excellent background to the conditioning of the European mind to imperialism.

Robinson, Jennifer, *The Power of Apartheid: State, Power and Space in South African Cities*, Oxford, Butterworth-Heinemann, 1996.

This is a remarkable and newly refreshing study of apartheid cast in postmodernist geographic thought about space and power. The author's contention is that the state depended on control and disposition of urban space.

Said, Edward, *Orientalism*, New York, Vintage Books, 1979.

Unquestionably the most significant writer on the cultural effects of dominant Western thought, Said traces the history of "orientalism" from the

Greeks to modern times. He argues that orientalism, the sweeping and enduring definition of those peoples east of Europe, has been a source of power to the West. This book has aroused much critical debate.

Said, Edward, *Culture and Imperialism,* New York, Vintage Books, 1994.

More ambitious in analysis and more sweeping in assessment, this volume asserts that modern European culture was largely formed in reaction to imperialism, conquest of the Other. Using the novel as a primary source of analysis, Said asserts that without imperialism there would have been no novel as we know it.

Solomos, John, *Race and Racism in Britain,* New York, St. Martin's Press, second edition, 1993.

Offering a general assessment that sweeps across the centuries, the narrative concentrates on the modern period and post-1945 developments. It is an excellent introduction to a very complicated problem.

Spurr, David, *The Rhetoric of Empire: Colonial Discourse in Journalism, Travel Writing and Imperial Administration*, Durham, N. H., Duke University Press, 1991.

This well-argued study offers a new view on the colonial experience as explained in European accounts. The chapters are arranged according to attitudes and perceptions to the formation of an imagined colonial landscape.

Young, Robert J. C., *Colonial Desire: Hybridity in Theory, Culture and Race*, London, Routledge, 1996.

An excellent and closely reasoned assessment of the mixture of cultures and their hybrid condition in the contemporary world.

Index